Table of Contents

Acknowledgments

The main lesson I learned in prison was gratitude. There have been so many people on this journey who have held out a hand to me and helped me along the way. Every woman at Estrella and Perryville who helped me when I was down and showed me a loving heart. Every staff member who saw me as a human being. I am deeply grateful.

Thank you to everyone who reached out to me from the real world when I was behind bars: my mother and best friend - Virginia K., my step-father - Michael K., my support - Paul R., my brother - Joe R., sister-in law - Angela M. my boss - Vic C. and several friends - too many to name.

Introduction
to the Journey

Most people never imagine they will go to prison. However, most people are in some kind of prison of their own making. Usually it is a prison of fear-fear of addiction, fear in a marriage, fear in a job, fear of loneliness, fear of change, fear of self. Everyone is doing their own kind of time. This is the story of my journey through prison and fear and the lessons I learned. I hope you will come to see them as valuable lessons wherever you might be .... *inside or out.*

Going to prison was the worst experience of my life. However, it is also the defining moment of my life. Prison has helped define who I am today as a human being and has given my life new meaning.

We never know what is at the end of a decision. No crystal balls. No Ouija boards. Something can seem disastrous and turn out to be a gift. Prison was a gift. It was not wrapped in a pretty blue box with a white satin Tiffany bow. I did not want to open it. It was an ugly, lonely, difficult, humiliating gift. I cried a lot. I hurt a lot. So why was it a gift if it was so awful? Good question. From the day I opened the box, I saw

4

things I wouldn't have believed possible if I hadn't experienced them myself. I saw abuse, abandonment, cruelty, despair, fear, neglect, disrespect, and apathy. From officers and from inmates.

I also saw compassion, kindness, respect, generosity, and love in many forms. From inmates and from officers. In prison, not everyone is evil, violent, and brutal, nor are they all sweet, kind and gentle. Prison is a microcosm of life, and the Bell Curve is alive and well in both inmates and staff.

My 8 months there was a journey, the worst and most difficult in a life full of journeys. I would not wish it on anyone, but I would not trade it. It enriched me in indescribable ways. I learned patience and compassion. I learned what to treasure and what to discard. I learned that the only way forward is through forgiveness and love.

Surely those things are gifts and I'm not sure how you learn them without a whole heap of adversity. Some people listen to my story and lament, if only this or if only that, then you wouldn't have gone to prison. Waste of breath. It's my journey. It's the journey I was meant to take. It has given me my passion and my purpose in life ... inside *and out.*

Preface

July 21, 2009 was the day that changed my life forever! My pride, my sanity, and my freedom would be taken away from me. It was the day I accepted the plea bargain the State of Arizona offered to me.

As I was getting dressed to go to court that morning, I became overwhelmed with emotions as I realized that I would not be coming home that day. I said goodbye to my dog, Roxy, and headed out the door not realizing what I was in for. My best friend, Paul, drove that morning. It was a cloudy, rainy morning; a reflection of what lay ahead.

We arrived at the Mesa Superior Court and waited in the parking lot for my family to arrive for support. Paul was a wreck. Such a wreck that he could not even bring himself to go into the courthouse to witness my fate.

I finally managed to get the strength to say goodbye to him. He held me and sobbed. As I exited the truck, my mother, my step father and uncle greeted me in the parking lot. I could see the sadness and fear in their faces. My mom held my hand as we walked through the glass doors of the courthouse.

We met with my attorneys to discuss what I am to expect upon accepting my plea. I was nervous, shaky and sick to my stomach. I wanted to cry so badly but needed to keep my composure for my mom's sake.

We entered into the courtroom and sat down on the hard, wooden benches. Not too long after, I was called up to the podium to face the judge and accept my fate. I was charged with four felonies as a result of two cases against me for credit card fraud and possession of a dangerous drug. The plea I agreed to was one year in Perryville Prison and two years probation upon my release.

I knew going into court that I would be detained and taken to Estrella County Jail, which is Maricopa County's jail for women, until my sentencing in 30 days. After reluctantly accepting my plea, I was immediately placed in handcuffs and escorted to more benches to wait for an officer to take me into custody. While sitting there, I exchanged loving glances and mouthed to my family... "I love you". Moments later I was taken out of the courtroom and placed into a holding cell.

Before I passed through the doors, I looked back at my family and waved goodbye. It was one of the saddest and most humiliating days of my life.

It became apparent to me immediately that once you are in the system, you are trapped, particularly in Maricopa County.

After about five or six hours sitting in the Mesa "holding tank" with one other girl who was there for the same crime, we are finally removed from the cell and placed into handcuffs and shackles which are placed on our ankles and led to the bus, which is named the paddy wagon. The bus ride seemed really long, though I am not sure of the duration from Mesa to downtown Phoenix.

We eventually arrived at our destination, which was the 4th Ave Jail run by Sheriff Joe Arpaio in Phoenix, affectionately known as "The Matrix" because it's a maze of hell.

I stood up and exited the "cage" I was sitting in on this dreadful journey. When the door finally opened, we were all instructed to follow the officer leading us into this cold, concrete building.

The shackles and handcuffs were removed and I was placed into a small holding cell with a filthy toilet and small sink attached to it. There were three other girls already in the holding cell when I entered. The holding cell was very small. After waiting for about ten minutes or so, the male officer called my name, "Stearns", and I was instructed to sit at a "window" to await medical questioning. The nurse took my blood pressure, took my temperature and asked if I was taking any medication. Shortly after, I was taken back to that cell.

Moments later, I was told by another officer to go to the end of the hall and sit down on the wooden benches against the wall and wait for my name to be called so I may have my mug shot and fingerprints taken. While sitting and waiting, I took in my surroundings and noticed that there were not more than maybe six other girls and the rest were men. On each side of me were men. A few of the men tried to make small talk with me, asking me questions such as, "Why are you here?" and comments of, "You don't look like you belong here". However, I was not in the mood to talk to anyone, especially tweaked out, drunk, smelly men. Half of which whom looked homeless.

This felt like a horrible violation, scanning my palms and sides of my hands digitally. Then regular prints with ink and paper.

I was asked, "Have you been here before?" One of 30 people before me and I am the only one to say no.

Once all the "formalities" were done, I was once again placed into another holding cell which was maybe 400 square feet, yet about fifty other women were in there along with me. It had to be well after midnight and I hadn't moved a muscle in over three hours. Many of the women in the "tank" had lied down on the filthy concrete floor hours ago and fell asleep. Most of them had their face a few inches away from someone else's butt; others were contorted in positions I've only seen circus acts do ... and me.. I was sitting on the edge of one of the benches with my legs crossed and head leaning against the wall. I hadn't slept in over 24 hours and was really tired but the phone hanging on the wall did not suffice for a pillow.

I would soon learn that most of the women in that "tank" had been in prison or jail at some point, just by listening to random conversations. I would also learn that prison was better than jail. The stories I listened to began getting way too depressing. I just tried to tune them out.

One thing to always remember, if you have not already experienced being arrested and being placed in jail at Maricopa County – dress warm and be prepared to wait a really, really long time.

Meanwhile, sometime around 12:30 am or 1:00 am, after getting absolutely NO sleep, they pulled me out of the "tank" with six other girls. We were led into this room where I was given a pink plastic bracelet with my mug shot and stats on it and a classification of "minimum". We were all then told to strip down, put our civilian clothes in a bag, and were given" stripes", which I would learn is the term for the jailhouse clothing; complete with the infamous pink socks, pink bra and rubber shower shoes, which were five times too big for me.

It was a relatively short bus ride over to Estrella Jail, though it was made longer by having full prison attire on for the first time. Here I remained for the next 32 days.

I had heard stories about what jails were like in Maricopa County, being run by Sheriff Joe Arpaio, but I never grasped the actual horror of what it was really like.

This is my account through my own experience of what county jail and prison was really like for women.

11

Chapter 1...Inside Out

July 2009. Inside Out, it's the way my life felt when I walked into my first jail. I was 38 years old, a well-educated, middle class woman suddenly face to face with another world. I was afraid, shocked and profoundly sad.

The first time they handcuff you is a shock. Some guards make them so tight so they cut your flesh at every move. Shackles are worse. They do what they are supposed to do; they restrict your steps and they are heavy and cruel on bare ankles. The holding cells are filthy, and there are only hard, concrete benches and an open toilet. At some odd hour, they bring salami sandwiches, but no trash bag so everyone just piles the trash on the floor. It helps feed the rats. They crowd about thirty-two women into an eight foot by twelve foot tank. Some are left to stand. No more room to sit or move. The theory is that this inhumane treatment will inspire people to not come back. It doesn't work. It just succeeds in dehumanizing them so they have no dignity or hope left.

I was kept there for over thirteen hours, waiting to be processed. Yes, 13 hours!!! In those 13 hours, I was detained at Court, transported to "intake", had fingerprints taken twice, 2 different locations, mug shot, given a pregnancy test (which was frustrating since I told 2 different people I could not have children). Nice waste of the county's money. Each time I was herded into another holding cell. Each cell was colder than the last one. Each cell was looking and feeling like a meat locker, since we were treated like cattle, might as well be cold for the slaughter. You quickly learn of those who had been in this facility before. These women were smart enough to wear the proper attire for the holding and herding process. Amazing enough, they wore 2 pair of pants, couple of shirts and most importantly socks. Yes, it was that cold – remember if you are ever arrested please dress accordingly - dress for the Arctic.

Finally, I was moved out to Estrella, the women's jail, with a group of other newbies. There our clothes were taken, we were strip searched, and given uniforms of black and white stripes with the red words "Unsentenced" printed on the back.

Upon my arrival to "intake" at Estrella jail, the real fun begins. I had never been to jail

13

before so the procedures were all new to me. I was placed into a small cell with several other women - most of which had the same long day I had.

So after waiting, and waiting, and waiting and still more waiting, I was given the jail handbook. I was asked to sign the back page and give back to the Correctional Officer (CO). I stupidly asked if I could read the handbook before I signed the acknowledgement page. I wanted to make sure I agreed with the finer points of my accommodations. I was told by the CO to read it on my own time because she had better things to do.

At this point, at least for me, I had been awake for about 18 hours. I was "slightly" tired. The CO handcuffed us and then tells us to grab our bag sitting next to the doors leading into the dorms down the halls. Do not forget, I was handcuffed, carrying a heavy bag down a long hallway as we were escorted to the dorms. When we walked through the door at the end, it was like walking into Dante's Inferno. Not what I expected since coming from the Arctic. I could feel the heat all the way down the hall. After being scared to death and tired – I did as I was instructed. As I struggled down the hallway with each companion, I was finally dropped off at "L" dorm. Upon my entrance into the dorm is where I learned what time it was. I learned it was 3:00AM!!

When we came through the doors of the dorm, the CO said to us, "I'm supposed to search you guys, but I'm not gonna. I'm supposed to, but I won't."

At the time, I was thinking "Oh just shut up and let's get on with it." Then I realized how the drugs got in. Through her and many like her. I cannot imagine anything more tedious than getting loaded in jail simply because you are essentially on your bunk 23.5 hours a day. You eat on your bunk, sleep and just ponder things.

By now I was past exhausted and only wanted to sleep. I really had no idea what to expect next. The dorm CO told me to go to bunk number XXX. I found my bunk, laid down the sheet (which I was previously given) on my mattress and finally climbed to the top bunk and placed my weary body as quietly as I could onto the bed. I looked over to my left and wondered what my bunk neighbor would be like; I hoped and prayed she would be nice. All of a sudden there was some movement from underneath a pink sheet, soon a head with long black hair raised from underneath, looked at me and said, "What the fuck"!

I would live to see another day.

One hundred twenty women in racks of bunks, two tiers high. Eight showers that didn't drain and eight toilets. One sheet, one blanket, no pillow, one uniform, one bra, one pair of panties, one pair of socks. Anything else is contraband. Anything else is country club. Everyone sweats and
smells and struggles to stay clean.

The first greeting as I headed to the restroom that next morning was a little doughy faced gang member wannabe who wanted to know if I smuggled in drugs.

"No."

She was visibly pissed and stomped off to ask the other girls I came in with.

The noise, the heat, the smell, the meanness of the guards, all contribute to a feeling of despair and fear. I didn't know a place could exist in the United States of America-the beacon of civilization for the rest of the world. I didn't want to believe that human beings could create this hell and others were willing to work in it.

Time feels upside down. The meals add to that. They do feed us in jail, if you can call what they are giving you to eat actual food. Let me give you the basics of breakfast.

First, I will discuss the most important meal of the day in County Jail, breakfast. Yummy!!!

Breakfast ALWAYS consisted of two loaves of wheat bread, two oranges, two half pints of Shamrock Farms fat free milk and two cookies. With the bread you are given turkey or 2 ounces of peanut butter. It's a tub of peanut butter - the peanut butter was fresh, there was a rumor that it was made fresh daily by the kitchen. If you got lucky, the bugs were caught up in the grinder and you did not see them as you ate. Yes, bugs!! Why do I know there are bugs in the peanut butter? Because sometimes they did not get ground up all the way. If you were lucky, you got a bug head included with yours or if you are really charmed...the whole bug. At least we get something to drink in the morning; 2 small cartons of milk and the milk was cold.

So, on to the oranges. As I understood, all the food was donated to the jail. A wonderful money saving tip from the Sheriff. So, with all the extra oranges around the city of Phoenix it is not a surprise that each and every breakfast included an orange. In the city of

Phoenix, our prime orange season is in early December through February. I was in jail in July and August. Love those oranges!

Then there are the cookies. At first they were some knock of brand of oatmeal creme pies. Later they gave us packages of six sandwich cookies. The white cookies could be filled with white cream, tan cream, yellow cream and on a rare occasion a pink cream.

In the jail, there are two meals a day and the food is always in the same perimeter: some type of fruit, some type of vegetable, tasteless beans or instant mashed potatoes and of course don't forget the best part ... the SLOP! It always tastes the same! Sometimes the slop is light brown. Sometimes it is more tan. Sometimes it is brown or dark brown. It's always a "brown" color and it always tastes the same. How can I describe what it looks like? Hmmmm ... I was asked that question and I thought about it. It's not quite liquid, but it isn't solid either. Have you ever had Campbell's Chunky Vegetable soup in the can? It kind of reminds me of that, if the vegetables were cut into smaller pieces, with some stringy stuff in it that I could never figure out exactly what it was and if it were mushier. So the tasteless mashed potatoes or the tasteless beans compliment the slop well then. The vegetables now ... well ... they are unseasoned, colorless, odorless and of course the recurring theme....TASTELESS! I tried to eat the broccoli once. I never tried again and I like broccoli. I bit into it and it gushed some foul water in my mouth. Oh, they do give us bread with dinner. Usually it is a croissant. One time it was two thick slices of white bread. They usually mush it down in your mashed potatoes or beans so when you go to pick up your nice, semi flaky croissant, half the bottom is stuck in your food. They don't give us anything to drink with your evening meal. Meals are served at irregular times, and time is twisted. Tock Tick, Tock Tick.

The morning meal is served in a plastic bag around 6am and the evening meal served around 6pm (these are rough estimates). I have never eaten everything in my bag until recently. I would eat half and give the other half away. Now I feel harassed for it. I swear not one day goes by without someone asking, "Do you have any extra bread?" 'Cookies?" Whether it's the person who sleeps next to you, under you or not even remotely near you. They all wander through the aisles begging for food. Even in the evening, "Does anyone have any bread they don't want?' "Butter?" Whatever you have, it's game to ask for it. They will take your tray and finish it off for you, or scoop that unwanted fruit right into theirs. Sigh! At least they ask.

It feels like a twenty first century concentration camp and, because of the heat, we are living in the ovens. Everyone in black and white stripes. Everything done to debilitate and demoralize. It is big business designed to create a revolving door of job security. Most inmates are poor. No one cares. The guards call everyone "Ladies," but their voices drip sarcasm and there is no place here for anything remotely lady-like.

I'm lucky; I've had a lovely life. I've worked and traveled. I know what love is. I have wonderful memories. Too many of these women have horrible memories. Too many have been abused by fathers, mothers, boyfriends, pseudo uncles. They do drugs to escape the pain. Then, to pay for their drug habit, they sell their bodies and steal. They are so young, but most are already mothers, and their children are scattered to the winds of family, adoption, or CPS (Child Protective Services).

The first week in the dorm, one of my neighbors literally shit herself all night long. I'd never seen such suffering and sadness. Heroin. Dear God, what an awful drug. I wondered how she could survive. The kindness of these drug-addicted women overwhelmed me. These women shared their few possessions with a generosity unseen in the world that I had known. I was profoundly sad and frightened, and they embraced and comforted me. They might be criminals to society, but their hearts were full of compassion. From these women, I learned that blessings can come from the least expected places and we should never judge.... inside or *out*.

Chapter 2...

Things I Took for Granted

SNACKS~ Well, who doesn't love snacks? They just aren't the same though when they're your basic livelihood of food. Every Monday they give you an order form where you can order snacks and hygiene items. You can order soda-7up, RC Cola, diet or cherry Coke, Welch's orange or grape, Squirt, Minute Maid apple, orange or cranberry juice and Dasani water. They have salty and sweet snacks like candy bars-Twix, Snickers, Hershey's, chips too. Whatever they want to give you such as Lay's, Doritos and Sun Chips. There are all sorts of things you can order ... tortillas, chili, tuna (in a bag), breakfast bars. The first week I could order I ordered a bunch of things. I had so many food items I managed to stretch them out over the course of two weeks. My supplies were dwindling though and I stressed that I would have to wait the following week to get anything else. You know, I LOVE CHOCOLATE! It's just not the same when I'm eating it to survive than when I'm eating it as an indulgence. Of course, I think it comes down to what they try so hard to take away here-enjoyment.

It's also hard to enjoy it when the 'moochers' are constantly on the prowl. These people love to take, without giving. They don't have anything to give either so I guess that's why. They'll get free postcards and try to trade for a food item. I didn't need a postcard. My family visited me. I was so paranoid my stuff would get stolen, which it can. I almost hated getting canteen items because I hated getting harassed for them. I've already given my bottom bunkie so much, and she's quick to take more. I used to get mad when I lived at home and someone would eat my snacks. I can't believe how selfish I was. At least at home I knew I would eventually get it back in return. Even then, it didn't matter because I loved those people, good people, generous people and I was happy to share with them. They've given me so much already!

MY BED~ Oh how I missed my bed and so many aspects about it. Sigh. My nice big fluffy, private, full of pillows bed! There were over 100 beds. They're bunk beds (ha, just when I thought I was done with bunk beds) all lined up. The bunk beds are lined up together so you're basically sleeping next to someone. In the room I was in, there were four rows of bunk beds next to each other. Down the middle of the rows they're divided so the officer can walk down the middle of the room. It's basically 46 beds in one row. They are single bunks. I was on the top bunk, second row from the end, in front of the showers. The other end from me is right in front of the bathrooms. All night I hear the toilets flushing and I smell everyone's business. I can never hear what the officer on duty is yelling because the showers and flushing of the toilets always drown them out. The bunks are metal, simple frames. They have skinny, flat, uncomfortable mattresses on top of them. You are given a very thin pink sheet to cover your mattress. If you are new here (which I was) you can always tell because you don't know how to keep your sheet from sliding off your mattress, luckily, the person next to me showed me how to tie the pink sheet on both ends so it didn't come off. You switch out your sheet once a week. You're given a big semi thick blanket to cover yourself. Luckily, it's not itchy, but it's not soft either. They switch that out once a month. NO PILLOWS! Sheesh. I was rolling seven pillows deep on my bed! I never in my life thought pillows was a luxury I couldn't have. So, there are beds all around you, and you basically live on them. I would spend about 90% of my time on my bed. I was lucky not to have a smelly bunkie. You keep all of your belongings on your bed. Since the mattress doesn't cover the whole bed frame, you can leave space on one end. This is where you store your things. Your towel, your canteen (food items ordered) and other personal items. I stored my items near the top of my head. I thought to do that so I could hear if anyone took anything while I slept. I only get off my bunk to shower, use the bathroom, visits or to get my daily exercise (which consisted of walking around and in between the rows of bunks). I couldn't wait to sprawl out on my bed ALONE and prop myself up with all of my pillows. Top bunks should be outlawed once you pass the age of 11!

HYGEINE ITEMS- You know, I thought I was lucky to have soft skin, clear skin, soft legs ... turns out it really does cost money to look good. All those things I named before are a result of me taking care of myself and being fortunate enough to have the products to do it. I was able to buy shampoo, conditioner, lotion, toothpaste ... but it's definitely not what I was used to. Suave doesn't cut it! I missed toothpaste that actually makes your mouth feel clean, lotion that keeps my skin soft. I was able to buy Neutrogena soap so at least I didn't smell like onions
anymore.

PRIVACY-Another thing I took for granted. Especially because I never thought I had any at home. Being in a room with over 100 girls didn't offer any privacy. The bathrooms are a little room with eight toilets, four on one side, and four on the other. They are separated by low wall dividers. The only thing that consisted of some sort of privacy was the curtain that was supposed to act as a door to the toilet room. It really didn't help. You go into the bathroom and there is always some girl or an officer that walks by and pulls the curtain back to check up in there. The showers aren't separated at all. It's another cement room with four showers on one side and four on the other. Sometimes, you may be able to steal a moment or two alone in there, but that's fleeting. It's never quite there. EVER! It reminds me of a school cafeteria; all cement, cold and noisy. It's noisy with the hum of 100+ girls chatting and laughing. Some are louder than others. I picked up people's stories here and there. It made me sad and wondered more than ever how I got there.

Chapter 3... Respect

What does that word mean? Oh, that. You won't get any of that in jail or prison. Of course, they treat you like animals. Being processed for the first time is the worst. The officers don't look at you. They just shepherd you around with stern and sour looks on their faces assuming you are scum and the worst of the worst. "Well you shouldn't have broken the law then." Yes. That is true, but I made mistakes...BIG ONES! I'm still a human being. Just human. Humans make mistakes. You can't tell me they have NEVER broken the law. Ever? They just didn't get caught. I did. Don't get me wrong, I know there are people out there who maybe never have broke the law, but you still shouldn't judge.

There is no respect on the outside and no respect in the dorm either. I already told you about the bunkie below me. I was continually harassed by her for food, as if I hadn't been generous enough. I had so little space to begin with and it was constantly being intruded upon.

The officers love to "toss" your bunk when you are gone, like when I was at visitation. They would rip through my stuff.

Chapter 4... Fear

It started in the jail where the incessant noise, violence, hostility, and indifference overwhelmed me. It is a hellish place for a healthy person. The black and white stripes and the conditions breed anxiety and stress. There are rules you don't even know about, and one hostile officer who is having a bad day can make yours miserable. I was brought up to respect authority and obey the rules, but these girls have no respect for anyone and will 'go off' on anybody.... inmate or guard.

There are lock-downs. There is pepper spray. There are brutal searches by the terrifying men in *black*. Why? Fights, drugs, who knows? I stayed on my bunk and read, read, read, read so that at least my mind can escape. The noise continues nightly until well past three in the morning and I long for silence. There is no silence. Instead, they yell at each other to be quiet. *"Shut up"*: *"No, you shut up"*: *"Shut the fuck up"*: *"No, you shut the fuck up, bitch "*.

And so it goes, night after endless night.

There were people there who I think found it physically impossible just to keep their mouths shut for five minutes. The chatter was almost always vulgar and littered with swear words. Actually, I should say polluted with swear words.

Here's the irony. Every night at ten as the lights go out, a prayer by an inmate starts. Lying on those hard, plastic mattresses, everyone says the Lord's Prayer together. Then this follows:

Now I lay me down to sleep, I pray the Lord my soul to keep. If I should die before I wake, at least it will be on video tape.

Then the real noise starts and goes all night.

Amen.

Chapter 5...Time

This is what my day consisted of...Wake up; lights on; get in line for chow; go back to sleep; wake up to shower; go back to sleep; wake up to read; wait for ID check; stay up; brush teeth; read; read; read; sometimes nap or stare at the wall; read; get dinner; read; brush teeth; lock down; lights off, wake up for midnight check and my day starts all over again.

That really put time in perspective for me. That had put a lot of things in perspective for me. All that time wasted on things that weren't important, people who weren't important. I was free to do whatever I wanted. But then I was locked up for 9 months.

Time....what I loved to waste so much of and what I could NEVER get back. I thought about all the things I would be missing. My freedom most of all. I had a couple of rough nights. I missed my family and most importantly, I missed my dog, Roxy. I was sad about my life, where it had taken me and where I ended up.

Big wrong, little wrong....WRONG is WRONG! Was I the only one who knew that in there? Was I the only one who felt remorse for what I had done? Why was I in there? Why was my lesson so hard learned? I was so scared of failure. How much more could I fail though? Life was already so hard. Why did I make it so much harder for myself?

I was never a nasty, mean person to begin with. However, it was quickly getting there. It started with cocaine and quickly escalated into meth. I'm lucky it stopped at meth, even though it consumed my well-being. I was 38 years old and I felt that I never really fit in-anywhere. I felt that way among family and friends. I was the background scenery while everyone else is a star. I didn't ever feel jealous-just alone.

Would I ever find the place where I belonged?

Chapter 6...

The Journey Begins

I remember the day I was taken to ASPC Perryville from Estrella County Jail. The bus picks up inmates who have been sentenced three days a week – Tuesdays, Thursdays and Sundays. I had been sentenced on a Thursday. Therefore, I was preparing to leave on Sunday. All day on Sunday, I was anxious and mentally ready to leave county jail and begin my "new adventure" down the rabbit hole. Imagine my disappointment when my name was not called that day. So, Tuesday arrives, again not leaving that hell hole. I begin to worry and become very annoyed. I was starting to think maybe I had been looked over somehow or that the paperwork had been screwed up. Thursday arrives. I was sitting on my bunk playing solitaire when the CO walks up to me and asks, "What is your name?" I replied, "Stearns". She asks to see my id and I show her. Then she says the words I had been longing to hear..."Roll up!"

Wasting no time, I jump off my bunk an ran over to another inmate I had befriended while I was there. I told her I was leaving and she cried. I asked her to call my best friend,

Paul, to let him know I was being transported to Perryville. As I am waiting for the CO to escort me out, she contacted Paul. He wanted to speak to me but I was not allowed to talk on the phone while waiting to be escorted out.

I had been up for 14-16 hours, in a tiny holding tank with 12 other women, no bench to sit on, no blankets, nowhere to sit but on the concrete floor. I sat in that tank all night, freezing, starving and so tired that I couldn't even think straight, a van finally picked us up and transferred us from the county jail to Perryville. I remember sitting in the van, chains on my ankles and cuffs on my wrists. Peeking out of the tiny corner of the window, I could see civilization. As the locals drove by, all wearing sunglasses, I examined their faces. I wondered what their everyday lives were like. Leaving Phoenix, shiny cars zipped past us. Drivers on cell phones became common. Housing developments and malls were replaced by rural scenery. When I realized I was leaving the town where I used to live, I felt sad. I longed to turn back the clock and be free again.

Eventually we arrived at the exit for Perryville. Then another sign warned: DO NOT STOP FOR HITCHHIKERS, ARIZONA

STATE PRISON. My anxiety went up. The van pulled up to the prison's main gate. I braced myself, as if I were getting onto a roller-coaster ride, for the types of things that happen when a fish arrives at a new prison.

A guard with a clipboard opened the side door. "What's your number?" she asked. I replied, "245745".

Upon given the all clear, we exited the van and the female officer instructed us to walk to the wall and stand by it. We march painstakingly to the concrete wall with our ankles still shackled. I take in my surroundings and notice a few inmates standing in the shade by a picnic table looking at us new "fish" while smoking their cigarettes. I felt like Andy Dufrain from the movie Shawshank Redemption, being sized up by the other inmates. At any moment they could yell out "New Fish, New Fish" like in the movie.

Chapter 7...

"R&A" Receiving & Admitting

After all of the inmates were accounted for, we were instructed to turn and face the wall. Our handcuffs and shackles were removed. We were then escorted to the Receiving & Admitting yard, aka R&A. Depending on how crowded it is, there are 2-3 women per 8' x 12' cell. Your custody level is determined at that point and you are assigned to either a minimum, medium or maximum custody unit. Currently at Perryville, there is one max unit (Lumley) which houses the max custody inmates, death row, suicide watch and the central detention unit. This is also where R&A is located. I was housed on Santa Maria unit which is a minimum custody unit.

We were given our State issued clothing upon our arrival to Perryville. This included one orange jumpsuit, 2 white sport bras, one pair long orange cotton shorts, one wash cloth, one towel, a cotton mauve pajama top shirt, two pair tube socks, underwear and a jacket. A jacket? Seriously? I arrived in August. The underwear, by the way, were the biggest underwear I had ever seen with the words written on the butt in bright orange letters... A.D.C. I couldn't help but laugh. We were also given two dark gray, heavy wool blankets and two sheets. Next we are provided our "indigent" personal hygiene kit which all new inmates receive. This includes a bottle of 4oz shampoo, small toothpaste, one travel size toothbrush, one deodorant (which is colorless, fragrance free, perfume free and dye free-WHY BOTHER?), three packages of shave cream BUT NO RAZOR, a bar of soap and lastly a small black comb. Really? A comb? But wait. It gets better. NO CONDITIONER AND NO LOTION. Yes, I repeat. NO CONDITIONER AND NO LOTION. I can't believe it.

So, I grab my "goody" bag which by the way is about 50lbs and carry/drag it over to the van that will be taking us to Lumley yard where R&A is. The officer instructs us to carry our own bags and place them into the van. This next part is a real kicker. After we place our bags into the van we assume we are to pile in right after. Hell NO! The van is to cart our shit over to the unit where we will be staying and we WALK. That's right, I said walk. Walk our tired asses across the hot dirt filled yard. We all look at each other with amazement and disgust.

After walking what seems like about ½ a mile, we finally arrive at our unit. The van is already there with the doors open. The CO tells us to grab our bags. Trying not to cry, I reach for my heavy bag and drag it out. As I am pulling it out, I lose my footing and I fall on the ground, landing on my knee. Looking around quickly in hopes that nobody saw me, I realized everyone saw me. I think my pride was more bruised than my knee was going to be.

We are marched into an air conditioned building where there are table and chairs. This is one of the buildings used for visitation on that yard which was Lumley. I later learned that this yard housed medium-maximum security inmates. An inmate awaited us while holding a clipboard. After we all manage to find a seat, the "clerk" begins calling our names (like roll call). We are given a bag which included a roll of toilet paper, sanitary pads, a Styrofoam cup and a small pencil. After orientation we head off to our yard, yard 28.

I was assigned cell number 266, upper tier. Each cell has 3 beds, a sink and a toilet. This would be my "home" for the next 2 weeks, bunked with 2 other inmates. One inmate was about 50 years old and the other was young, she spoke Spanish only. I was assigned the middle bed. After glancing around the cell for "inspection", I noticed the floors look dirty; the walls were painted a pale yellow (which was worn and paint missing), vandalism on walls from prior inmates, 2 oblong cork boards (covered in what looked like dots of white toothpaste). Toothpaste is also used as a "glue" to hold up pictures, cards, letters, etc. One of the boards was half torn off. The shelve and door are painted a bluish gray color. The floor was much worn, but it looked like it was once painted a royal blue. The bed mattress...if you can call it that-more like a yoga mat...was dried and cracked.

Now remember, the cells are only 8' x 12'. We are locked into our room 23 hours a day, every day, until we are moved to our assigned yard. I was in that cell for almost 2 weeks. When the CO walked away she said, "Welcome to hell ladies". Our cell is metal and concrete-very industrial chic. Every day for one hour we are allowed out of our cell to do whatever we want. Most of us girls take this time to shower. I had NO idea how gross a shower could be! It is mandatory we wear our shower shoes each time we shower. Hmm. I wonder why?

A short time later, another officer walks by our room and yells, "Get in compliance and get ready for chow"! Being properly dressed (or in compliance) means jumpsuit, shirt, socks, and shower shoes. Hair must always be pulled up or back in a ponytail. NEVER DOWN. Our ID clipped to the left side of our jumpsuit too.

We all march and stand next to our cell door outside and wait for the go ahead from the officer. While walking to the kitchen, I take in my surroundings. There is a chain link fence with two types of barbed wire around the entire perimeter of the prison. A camera which watches us 24/7, a tower where the officers keep watch from, several trash cans and a few concrete benches.

At this point we are all standing in the hot Arizona sun in the middle of a concrete yard in 110 degree weather wearing two layers of clothes and tube socks. Holy SHIT I felt like I was going to pass out. As I walked through the kitchen door, a burst of cool air hits my face. I close my eyes for a moment and try to imagine I am anywhere but there.

Suddenly, a deep voice yells at me, "What is your name?" I show him my ID. He hands me a receipt and then hands me an orange plastic tray. I round the corner to the dining area. Each table seats 4 inmates. I follow the inmates in front of me, set my tray on the table and pick up a yellow cup and walk over to get something to drink. The choices were pink lemonade, water, tea or fruit punch. Somedays you only get one choice. I guess it was my lucky day.

We were served a chef salad, jello, bread and butter. I began eating slowly to savor each bite. Looking around the room, I noticed everyone "inhaling" their food. We only had 5 minutes to eat our food. I hardly made a dent in my food and went to bed that night starving.

I survived my first day in prison. Later that night as I lay in bed I stare out the small oblong window which faced the desert. In the distance I could see the lights of cars racing down the I-10 freeway. My eyes filled with tears as I fought back crying out loud. I whispered..."I love you mom, Joey, Sierra, Dylan, Paul, Angela, Roxy and even my ex-husband, Scott, for whom I blamed for me being there.

Chapter 8...

Cleanliness is Godliness

In prison, neatness counts. There are rules and policies for everything. The Arizona Department of Corrections (ADC) policy manuals take up a complete six-foot shelf in the Deputy Warden's office. Our living area falls under this. Everything has a designated place, and we are provided a handy diagram so there is no question of proper compliances. I had the top bunk. Where I put my toothbrush, my hygiene products, my TV (if I had one) are all spelled out. There are places for towels, laundry bags, commissary items, and legal boxes. No creativity allowed.

The room is about six feet by eleven feet. If my roommate and I both need to dress at the same time, it's tight quarters. There is only one chair and it is part of the step-ladder to get up to what I call my 'Penthouse'. Climbing up isn't easy either. These rooms were built to be singles and then, somewhere along the way, overcrowding demanded double bunking and that has turned out to be hazardous.

First, getting up and down is dicey. The small ladder stands straight up and is designed for gymnasts who are at least 5'6" tall.

Storage is another challenge. Each of us is assigned a three foot by three foot drawer for all of our clothes. We don't have much, but it's enough to fill a drawer. We are also allowed three legal boxes for legal papers, books, and mail.

This tiny room functions as our living room, dining room, bedroom, kitchen, and bathroom. Our bathroom sink is also our kitchen sink because we do cook, but that's another story. So, what about the bathroom and privacy? There is none. Any sensitivity you have is left behind with your first strip search. However, I had made up a rule. In our room we had an imaginary door around the toilet. When one of us was on the throne, the door is shut and we have total privacy. We're all pretty considerate and this works very well. I did long for the day when I'll have a real bathroom again, but in the meantime, I have one in my imagination.

'All areas must be free of dust and dirt,' says the policy. That's impossible here, but we try. Perryville sits in a huge dirt field where dust witches are constantly on attack. Almost daily the winds swirl around us, covering everything in a fine layer of grime. One window is stationary and not designed to open, but the other is supposed to open about three inches for ventilation. The room is all gray steel and cream concrete. There is no softness.

I didn't object to the policies. It saves arguments when roommates aren't as agreeable as Lynn and I were. It's the softness and color I missed. And I have to agree that neatness does count. It's like living in a shoebox; unfortunately, one from Payless, not from Barneys. The room feels bigger and better when everything is tidy and put away.

Below is a picture of the cell's at Perryville Prison.

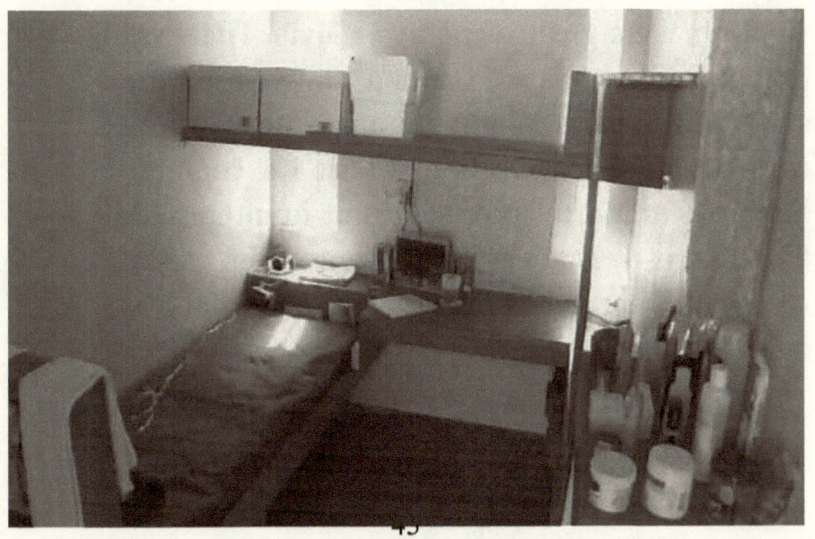

Chapter 9...Mail Call

Do you remember when people used to write letters on elegant stationary with matching envelopes? Do you remember cards you could actually hold instead of e-mail ones? Before e-mail, way back even before telephones, letters were magical links between families, friends, and lovers who poured out their emotions on paper. Getting a letter was a special occasion.

Mail Call is an important event in prison. Every day at 4:15 in the afternoon, our mail is distributed. The C.O. (Corrections Officer) stands at the picnic table in front of our pod and, as the doors open by Central Control, we all come out into the sunshine, blinking at the brightness after the gloomy light of our cells. It would make a great scene in a movie. The vivid orange uniform is in striking contrast to the stark gray walls. Women lounge against the rails upstairs. Downstairs, we sit on concrete benches, trying to look cool and uninterested, like this really isn't very important, when all the while our hearts beat faster as we pray that our name is called.

Some names are called often, almost daily. They are the ones blessed with family and friends who care. Some names are never called. Because they have no one, they rarely leave their bunks for mail call. It is just not worth the effort and the inner humiliation. Every afternoon at 4:15, they are reminded that nobody cares.

That's what a letter is in prison. It's an envelope of hope. It says that in the midst of the outside hustle and bustle, someone has taken the time to stop and acknowledge you as a person. It's a validation of you as a human being, courtesy of the U.S. Mail.

Mail Call is a powerful life lesson for me. It reminds me of what is really important in life ... family, friends, and loved ones. It also reminds me how powerful a letter is and how meaningful it is to receive one behind bars. Postcards, greeting cards, magazine articles, books, magazines. Those cards and letters touch us on many levels, especially the pictures and drawings from children. They open doors to endless possibilities.

Recently, I was stunned to learn that the local Sheriff, who prides himself on being the toughest sheriff in the country, decided to restrict the mail in "his jail." No envelopes are allowed in or out of his facility except legal mail. Postcards only. If it can't fit on a postcard, too bad. No more family photos, no drawings by your children, no love letters, no interesting articles. The Sheriff said that sorting the mail was too labor intensive and a security threat, but this approach only adds to the desolation, despair, frustration, and bitterness. Bear in mind that many of these inmates are awaiting trial, haven't had their innocence or guilt established, and can be there for months or even years. They are treated as guilty when the rule of law says innocence is presumed. For inmates, it is cruel and unusual punishment and does not contribute to rehabilitation in any way.

Mail is valued in the outside world. Statistics show that less than three percent of our mail now is personal. Ninety-seven percent of the mail we receive is junk or bills. Think of the power of sending a real letter. Think of a person you would like to touch emotionally. If you are reading this book, perhaps you know an inmate. Put the book down and write them a letter instead. Or if you don't know an inmate, just send a card to someone you care about. Not an e-card, a real one. You are sending an envelope of hope and I promise you will touch a life. That is a powerful thing to do ... *inside or out.*

Chapter 10 ...

Prison Cuisine & Inmate Recipes

Prison fare isn't fair to anyone. People say it's unidentifiable, but they're wrong. I can identify all of it. It is mostly texturized vegetable protein either formed into soy-edified patties of various shapes and sizes or loose and sanguineous "slop", which comes in different flavors and colors for each day of the week.

In prison, food is more than a pastime or a preoccupation; it is a passionate obsession for almost all of the inmates. I was not one of them. I do enjoy good food but I am what others call a "picky" eater. I have always seen food as nourishment, not a hobby, artistry or sport. Cereal for dinner or cold pizza for breakfast never left me dissatisfied.

One of probably hundreds of death ransoms presented to me by women who wanted a snack, this type of incident always pissed me off. It embarrassed me to see women behaving like that, so desperate and so desirous of such utter crap. Going out in search of food in such a debased way seemed so primitive, so carnal to me that I almost felt an evolutionary setback happening around me, putting homo sapiens back to times when the hypothalamus- the gland that controls one's appetite- was so underdeveloped that it had to fire constantly to remind those cretins to keep eating in order to stay alive. *They all couldn't be this hungry!*

I should've been more compassionate toward those women because the reasons for their behavior are multiple and sad. First, many women came to prison after prolonged "runs" – periods of occasional homelessness, probable substance abuse, definite chaotic behavior and absolute anorexia. They have, somewhat comfortably, not eaten a full or functional meal in months. Second, because drug use usually ceases in the relative safety of incarceration, another addiction often takes place – an addiction to food. Many of the same behaviors associated with substance abuse rear themselves on the day commissary bags fall into the inmates' anxious clutches: stealing, lying, secretive bingeing, bargaining, prostituting and eschewing one's usual responsibilities, even if those responsibilities are only to brush one's teeth, wash one's face and make one's bed every day.

Potluck is a tradition in prison. Everyone brings a dish to show off her culinary skills, a huge challenge here. Inmates are allowed to buy a very limited array of food items from the company store. Almost everything available is junk. Lots of chips and candy, but only three items of protein: peanut butter, tuna, and beans. These make up the bulk of our menus. What can you do with junk food? The creations are amazingly good, but ultra high in carbs and calories.

My hors d'oeuvres are a hit. I made cheesy tuna roll-ups -- tuna, mayonnaise, cheese, and jalapenos rolled up in tortillas. I cut them into bite size pieces using our cutting tool, the edge of our very small plastic mirror. No knives allowed. I even made a serving tray by painting and decorating the bottom of the box that brownies come in, lining it with a pretty magazine ad. Not exactly hygienic, but certainly pretty. The roll-ups are served with a tasty sauce made from squeeze cheese, mayonnaise, and powdered milk. No seasoning allowed, but somehow inmates find a way. Also, I learned how to make a yummy sour cream and onion cheese dip. Take a bag of Sour Cream and Onion Potato Chips and crush them to a fine texture. (Keep them in the bag and use a water bottle as your rolling pin.) Using the bag as your mixing bowl, add three packages of squeeze cheese, powdered milk and jalapeno juice to taste. Consistency should be creamy. Serve in a bowl with tortillas or crackers. Don't ask about the calories.

For the main course, the tables are set with our beautiful prison china, white plastic bowls filled with various delicacies. We're only allowed one small bowl so cooking is a challenge. Most inmates actually have two bowls, but the second one is contraband and on quarterly shakes, the C.O.'s routinely throw it away. So then everyone buys a new one for twenty-five cents. It gives the company store more business and inmates then have two bowls for the next three months. It's a prison game everyone plays. The highlights of the main course are creatively called Pasta with Tuna and Sour Cream Chicken. Do not consider making these unless you are rail thin, have ridiculously low cholesterol, and just love junk food, because it is indeed junk food.

After we've eaten much more than our stomachs are used to, desserts are forthcoming. One inmate has dazzled us with a delicious chocolate cake made from candy bars. I made chocolate mint truffles, lots of work, but well worth it; easy to serve and bite size. I too decorated a brownie box for serving. In an ugly place, we appreciate the efforts to make things pretty. It is a wonderful day when we can celebrate and practice the little niceties of life. We are isolated in such an ugly place, but we use our creative energy to produce a pretty party to share with our friends. It's the closest thing possible to normal behind the razor wire. It lifts our spirits and brings laughter into our lives. No matter where you are or what your circumstance, remember that you are a creative spirit with much to contribute and share. Sharing that creativity and joy will give meaning to your life ... inside or out.

BELIEVE IT OR NOT RECIPES

These are Surprisingly Delicious and Completely BAD for You

Sour Cream & Onion Chicken 2 Bowls

Small amount of milk (pilfered from somewhere)

2 pouches of chicken in gravy (mostly gravy)

1 bag Sour Cream &: Onion Potato Chips (finely crush chips in the bag using a water bottle)

Grilled potatoes pilfered from breakfast

Chopped jalapenos

Boil 1 cup of water with a stinger. Pour into bowl, and immerse pouch of chicken & gravy. Heat up about 3 minutes.

Pour 1 bag crushed chips in 2nd bowl. Add warm chicken and mix well.

Add some potatoes and keep mixing. Add chopped jalapenos to taste and some milk to smooth consistency.

Repeat with the 2nd pouch.

When it's all mixed well, combine the bowls. Then wash out the empty bowl and line with Saran Wrap. Add all the mixture to this bowl, pressing tightly to make a mound.

Turn out on a serving box you've decorated with pretty magazine ads and covered with Saran Wrap you've pilfered from somewhere. Decorate the mound with whole chips and surround it with crackers. Alternatively, you can roll it up in tortillas and serve.

Chapter 11... Language

Have you listened lately to how people speak our language? I don't mean what Katie Couric says on the nightly news. I mean what your neighbor, your spouse, a teenager, or the kids next door are saying. Sometime in the last century, not so long ago, the F word was considered really, really bad, truly the worst obscenity in our vocabulary. If you said that, people knew you were serious. How times have changed.

Remember Gone with the Wind? When Scarlett O'Hara Butler realizes her husband Rhett Butler is leaving her, she cries out to him in anguish, "Where shall I go? What shall I do?"

As he puts on his fantastic Panama hat, he looks straight at her and says, "Frankly, my dear, I don't give a damn."

Millions read these lines in the best-selling novel, but Hollywood had a fierce battle with the censors to allow damn in the movie. Until then, damn simply wasn't heard on the silver screen. Once damn was uttered, Pandora's Box was opened and anything was possible. Of course, that was in 1939. It took about thirty-five years to allow the F word. I think M*A*S*H started it, and now it's almost a miracle to see a movie without it.

Walk along the street, stand in a line at the supermarket, or visit a schoolyard. You'll be stunned. It's not used for emphasis in dramatic situations; it's become a ubiquitous verb, adverb, and adjective. Half the words in a sentence can start with F.

We seem to be numb to it. No one really hears it anymore. But the children hear it. They hear it in the movies, in the kitchen, in the car, and in the living room. The movies and television are full of it; bad language and bad attitude. Two and a Half Men is training a little wise guy. The Simpsons is a lesson in how to insult people. The list is endless and sarcasm wins the day, always at someone's expense. It's one thing for adults to watch, aware that this behavior isn't acceptable at the office. It's another for kids to watch and think it's cool. They hear and they copy - to be like the big kids, like mom and dad, like the movie stars. We're creating another generation of foul-mouthed, sarcastic, negative people. I used to swear back when it was still shocking and I did it for shock value. It was very effective.

Then my eyes were really opened. I came to prison where the language simply left me speechless. There are so many young women who cannot speak without using this word. Honestly, if we made it impossible to use, I think they'd all be mute. It's become as common as a "fucking coke" and "fucking fries." And it's extremely limiting. The only way they know how to insult each other is with this basic four letter word.

"Fuck you."

"No, fuck you."

"I fucking said fuck you, bitch."

They throw it back and forth like a ping-pong ball and it would be really comical if it weren't so sad. The truth is we have created a monster of free speech. And what is free about it? In the long run, it's very expensive. It costs us our manners, our civility, our vocabulary, our creativity, and our love. If we are throwing vulgarities at each other like big clods of dirt, we have no time to be gentle, kind, and loving. The words sound aggressive and they are.

I like words like puppy and tapioca; they make me smile. Words like daffodil and sunshine fill me with light. Words like love and hope fill me with joy. Using happy, positive, optimistic words can become just as much a habit as nasty, negative ones. So, I decided to stop swearing completely (ok, maybe cut it down) and I practice using happy words. Surprisingly, my language seems to impact others and I notice less swearing in my vicinity. (Or is it my age?) Whatever it is, I appreciate that my behavior acts as a positive influence and that inspires me to keep it up. Everything in life requires practice so my practice might as well be positive, a good habit to maintain ... *inside and out.*

Chapter 12...

Pizza and Sunshine

Four days and a wake up. Three days and a wake up. Two days and a wake up. The countdown began three weeks earlier when the announcement shook the yard. Inmates will be allowed to buy pizza for charity. Pizza Hut will sell the prison large pizzas for $6. The prison will add a $4 contribution for Special Olympics. For $10, we will get Pizza Hut delivered to our prison door, all for charity.

This tantalizing possibility has been dangled before us for months. I heard that last year an inmate committee was appointed and they took orders for 1400 pizzas. Anticipation soared, then all hopes were shattered. The accounting department said it would be too much work, and the catering service concession said they would lose money because no one would eat in the cafeteria. To a chorus of I told-you-so's, cynicism prevailed. So, when this new announcement came, we exercised cautious optimism, placed our orders, and began the countdown.

Nothing in prison is easy. The logistics of this exercise require endless meetings, false starts, changes, and many nay-sayers.

"Inmates don't deserve anything special."

"We're too short staffed."

"The bookkeeping will be a nightmare."

"We can't maintain security and there will be a riot over the pizza."

Each argument was gradually overcome with the overriding cry: "It's for charity."

The inmate committee took the orders for cheese or pepperoni. Each inmate account had to be checked and double checked to make sure there was indeed enough money in the account to cover the expenditure. Lists were counted and recounted because inmates are constantly being moved to other yards or back to court. Nothing was left to chance. And up until the last minute, we held our breath, knowing they could still change their mind. We breathed easier when we heard the check had actually been sent to Pizza Hut. Hope sprang out all over again.

Finally, the big day arrives, bright and clear, actually just another of our endless Saturdays. Breakfast at seven, girls working out, playing cards, doing laundry, and getting ready for much anticipated visits. All ears, however, are focused on the radio chatter. At nine a cheer goes up when we hear that the ADW has gone to the front gate to receive the pizza delivery trucks.

We patiently wait until 10:30 when the order comes. Lock it down. Never have we moved so quickly to our rooms, happy to slam those doors and wait some more. Finally, through the narrow window, I can see the truck drive up, followed by inmates carrying tables and chairs, trailed by the supervisory staff. Soon the tables are piled high with pizza boxes. Pod by pod, the doors are unlocked and women line up to receive their boxes and be checked off. I generously bought pizza for my roommate and myself, one cheese and one pepperoni. Back in our room, the door slams shut for eleven o'clock count, and my bunkie and I are alone with fresh, hot pizza. We are giddy with excitement. First, we examine the boxes, appreciating the bright red color in our drab little room. We actually read all the copy before opening the box to marvel at the beautiful pizza so artistically arranged. Actually, it's just normal pizza cut into normal slices like we've all eaten hundreds of times outside. But we aren't outside, and for many, it's been years since they have seen Pizza Hut. Try to imagine that.

The rich, saucy, cheesy smell fills our tiny room as we make a momentous decision - pepperoni first. Never has a pizza tasted so good. We chew slowly, savoring each bite, dissecting the individual flavors: real tomatoes, real cheese, and real pepperoni. In between chewing, we giggle, we laugh, we jump up and down. I'm not sure why we feel such joy, but it is heady and infectious. It is partly the pizza. It is scrumptious. But it is also the joy of having such a special treat, such an unprecedented, previously forbidden event behind bars. At noon, the doors open and we prepare for a little al fresco picnic in the warm autumn sun. But there are more treats in store. We all look at each other in stunned silence when we hear the announcement, "All yards are open for one hour." The Santa Maria yards are kept separated through a convoluted system of scheduling so this is unheard of. (This unprecedented treat comes from our Deputy Warden, who always sees inmates as human beings and is an optimist at heart.) It takes a few minutes for the news to sink in, but gradually we head for the gates and the main recreation field. Everyone is out laughing, jogging, sharing pizza, and visiting with friends. We are very grateful for this surprising treat and for the Deputy Warden's faith in us. I stroll with Stephanie and

Vanessa, and then stop to see Charlotte ("Smiley").

The giddiness continues over such luxuries. It's rather like a street fair without the hippy artists and food booths. I want to actually sit on the grass, so I walk to the middle of the field and sink down in the greenest spot I can find. (Remember this is Arizona, so it's not exactly lush.) I'm hoping for softness, but fat chance. It is actually very prickly, with lots of busy ants. I don't care. I lean back to soak up the soft sunlight and watch the parade. The women, bright orange Halloween pumpkins, laugh and chatter while the guards in their drab brown uniforms stand silently, eyes moving, watching for the slightest hint of trouble.

Of course, there is none. We all know that one tiny misstep can shut this down and ruin any future possibilities.

Anyone who dares act up will incur the wrath of the entire inmate population. But all is calm and all is very bright. We are simply too full of pizza and joy to act up. Besides the $5,000 raised for Special Olympics, there was more generosity. There are many inmates who are indigent, without family support, and even if they're lucky enough to have a job, it only pays ten cents an hour. There was no way they could afford pizza. But inmates like myself and all the others too numerous to name bought extra pizza to give away. No one went hungry on this special day. Sharing is a big thing inside. Nobody has much, but what they do have is shared. I've seen more generosity inside from criminals with nothing than I ever saw outside from people who have everything. Why is that? I think it comes from pain and heartbreak. When you really suffer, something transformational can happen. You realize you don't want anyone to hurt the way you have. So, your compassion increases and with compassion comes generosity. One lovely day in October in prison, all hearts were mended, full of love and joy over something so simple, so abundant outside, pizza and sunshine. The next time you have pizza, think about how you can share something of yourself with the rest of the world. There are many ways to share and many hearts that need mending. If women in prison with nothing can find something to share, so can you. I know your generosity can make a difference ... *inside or out*.

Chapter 13...

The Rabbit Hole

Sometimes in prison I feel like I am Alice and I have fallen down the Rabbit Hole into Wonderland. There is a brown queen yelling, "Off with her head. Send her to the hole." There are all manner of brown palace guards to protect the queen and do her bidding. And the mad tea party goes on endlessly. So often, there are no rational explanations for things, so it must be Prison Wonderland. One day a C.O. tells Lynn that she has to turn in her appliances. Lynn is shocked. Turning in appliances means loss of privileges and this is connected to a ticket. She has no ticket. She knows it's a mistake. Also, it is Super Bowl weekend and Lynn is a huge sports fan. She tells the C.O. it's a mistake. "Too bad," he says. "You still have to turn in your appliances and you can get it straightened out on Monday." Lynn wants to speak to a sergeant, our right in case of a dispute. Very displeased, the C.O. radios his sergeant that the inmate is refusing to turn in her appliances and demanding to speak to him. "Okay, send her up," the sergeant says. At the yard office, the sergeant checks the computer and sure enough, Lynn is ticket-free. It is a mistake. She doesn't have to turn in her appliances, but the sergeant issues her a ticket for refusing to obey a direct order to turn in her appliances - that she didn't have to turn in the first place. Yes, it was a mistake, but since she refused to obey the mistake, she gets a ticket and loses her TV after all. Staff is paranoid about direct orders. If a C.O.gives you a direct order, no matter how outrageous it may be, if we disobey it, we get a ticket. In a rational world, the sergeant would have acknowledged the mistake and sent Lynn on her way, maybe even apologized. That's out of the question in prison. Now here's the clincher. When Lynn goes to the disciplinary hearing, she gets a little lecture and the ticket is dismissed. It was a lot of paperwork for nothing, but that's how things work in Prison Wonderland. Inmates are not allowed to carry anything in their pockets to work except tobacco and toilet paper. Say you're trying to quit smoking and want to carry some hard candy. Nope. Cigarettes are okay; hard candy is not. Chap Stick? Forget about it. A pen to use at work? Nope, they should be furnished (but they aren't). What about diabetics and hypo-glycemics? Can they carry candy? Nope. Well, maybe. No one seems to agree on that one.

Soup cups are another Prison Wonderland game. The store sells this Ramen-like soup in Styrofoam cups. We re-use the cups in all manner of ways. We put our cheap plastic official cup in it so the Styrofoam one becomes an insulator. It keeps the official cup from sweating all over our fine steel furniture. We use it to boil water with our stinger so we won't burn our hands when we pick up the hot cup. It's also an extra serving bowl in a pinch. They're very handy. But at every shake, the empty Styrofoam cups are gleefully tossed. They seem to be a red flag. One C.O. told me they were a good hiding place. Good grief, these girls are more ingenious than that.

As long as they sell the soup, inmates will be using those cups. During the shakes, they toss them out in the morning, and by noon everyone has a new one. It's a Prison Wonderland game. Bartering and trading, which is against ADC policy, is another Wonderland game. It's another red flag. When I arrived, I was indigent; no money, no job, no nothing. But the C.O. at State Issue (where we are given our prison wardrobe) said I must turn in the shower shoes I was issued at R &, A and buy the $65.00 ones from the prison store. How am I supposed to do that without job or money? I think with horror that I will have to go barefooted, a guarantee for athlete's foot in the grimy showers. One of the inmate clerks who worked at State Issue offers to buy the shower shoes for me, right in front of the officer! We've been warned that this is considered bartering and trading. Even worse, she wants me to be in her debt. I am painfully green as grass. I look around for help. The officer nods her head in agreement. "Come back next week", she says, "and be ready to exchange shoes." Her tone is commanding. I do as I am told. I return and exchange shoes, all with the unofficial blessing of one of the strictest C.O.'s on the yard. Welcome to Prison Wonderland. They bend the rules to suit. The bartering and trading rule is ridiculous, particularly on a female unit. Women don't barter, they give and giving is forbidden. I was penniless for several months when I first arrived, and I'll never forget the generosity of these women I didn't even know. They were gifts. But, if a C.O. had been in a bad mood, we could all have been ticketed.

Prison Wonderland is full of convoluted rules. Often, they only succeed in causing confusion, bad morale, and a lot of unnecessary paperwork. There is no doubt that there are some bad women in prison who look for trouble and seem to delight in breaking the rules, but the majority are confused, frightened, and just want to do the best they can to get out of here with their sanity intact. There are a lot of rules and punishments for the first group, but absolutely no rewards for the latter. There are no honor dorms, no trustee jobs, no increases in privileges if you're good. It's one size fits all and the result is a sort of negative apathy. Why try? Why bother? Inmates think, nothing I do matters in Prison Wonderland.

One person can make a difference, even in prison, even against razor wire odds that many say are insurmountable. Truly, sometimes they are, but not always. Sometimes, when you have a vision, you just have to stay focused against the odds, swim upstream, and ignore the naysayers. I don't know why people want to rain on other people's parades, tearing down ideas and destroying dreams. Think how difficult it is to compose a symphony, write a book, or paint a picture, and how easy it is to criticize it. Critics are a dime a dozen, especially in Prison Wonderland, but we don't have to join them. We can be builders, doers, and dreamers anywhere. We can make a difference because what we do does matter ... *inside or out.*

Chapter 14...

Mega Shake

The buzz spread across the yard like a swarm of bees, loud and fierce. A major shake is coming, a nightmare shake to end all shakes. Why? We just had our quarterly shake a month ago. This, however, is a statewide shake ordered by the Director after serious contraband was found at Florence Prison. What was found remains a mystery, but rumor has it that weapons, a cell-phone, and a laptop were found. A laptop! Really? Whatever they found sparked enough interest to schedule this mega-shake and our day is fast approaching.

At Perryville, rumor is king, or should I say queen? The rumors come at machine gun speed. The Men in Black are coming. They are like a SWAT team. They'll be yelling and screaming and using intimidation tactics to scare us. They'll destroy the rooms. They'll turn our storage boxes upside down and dump everything on the floor. The dogs are going to walk all over our beds. They are going to rip open our food items. I am horrified.

Let me explain the emotions of a shake.

Inmates are among the most creative pack rats on the planet. Because we aren't allowed much, more is definitely better in an inmate's world. What we own would embarrass a homeless person - an extra white plastic spork (a weird, non-dangerous combination of spoon and fork for the inmate population), a Styrofoam soup cup, the extra bowl and cup we manage to hide for cooking tasks, an extra plastic pill bag for candy, an empty peanut butter jar to keep candy away from the bugs. It's all junk, but it's our junk and it helps keep our world tidy. It is also contraband. A peanut butter jar is only allowed when it has peanut butter in it. Once it's empty, using it for candy is forbidden. Same with the soup cup; in prison, recycling is not allowed.

Then there is the problem of extra books and magazines. I constantly chaff at the severe restriction of five magazines and seven books. It is my only sin in prison. I always have too many. It never ceases to amaze me that a place exists in the United States of America where books are seriously restricted. Extra books are contraband, and I must find places for them. I farm mine out to the girls who don't read. They are happy to keep my cherished books and once the shake is over, back they come. My contraband is simple.

The old numbers have more serious stuff that they have stashed God knows where; tweezers, needles, cigarette lighters; all forbidden, all treasured, and all here.

In Arizona, all prisons have a quarterly shake. Inmates are locked down for the day as yard by yard, room by room, we are searched. It's supposed to be a surprise, but it never is. The word comes down through the inmate grapevine and Spring Cleaning commences. Prized contraband is tossed or hidden and by the time Shake Day arrives, we are ready.

Prepped or not, inmates hate shakes. It's disruptive and invasive, but that's prison. So, when we hear the announcement for C pod to get ready, we dutifully march out to the fence and line up while the dogs sniff us and the officers ransack our cells. Then it's over for three months and we get more soup cups and sporks, we retrieve our books, and things go back to normal.

Until now, the mega-shake. They are going to look for hidden weapons in all the nooks and crannies. This is a set-up waiting to happen. If someone doesn't like you (inmates or staff), they can sneak in your room and hide something outrageous like a needle or a shank. To be safe, we look under the bunks and behind the drawers and shelves just in case there's something hidden from years ago. I reorganize my storage boxes and farm out my books. I am ready.

Shake Day dawns. The bus of extra C.O.'s arrives very early, and they start at the other end of the yard. That means we will be last. My heart pounds until I realize I am being ridiculous. God said, "Fear Not" and there is no reason to be afraid. It's just stuff and pitiful stuff at that. I survived Estrella, under nightmarish conditions. God has always been with me and I know I can do this. I pray over the room and settle down for the long wait.

We are locked down for thirty-six hours, during which time we get ADC room service; what the girls euphemistically call "bag-nasties" (yucky sandwiches, a bag of stale chips, and a dry cookie). Many women go slightly stir-crazy. I am perfectly content reading, writing, drawing and coloring. My roommate Lynn sleeps or plays cards. She is without a doubt the best sleeper I have ever seen. She can sleep for days through noise and light. If there was an Olympic category for sleeping, Lynn would win the Gold. I am envious.

Finally, at 9:45 the next day, we hear the bullhorn for C pod. I am ready. I have stripped my bed, emptied my drawer and folded everything neatly on top of the desk.

The doors pop open and we are called out very professionally. Surprise. There is no yelling and the officers are in regular brown; no black in sight. We are almost politely escorted to a corner room to be strip searched. We are then walked over to a chair which is also an X-ray. You sit on the chair and it's supposed to scan your body to find any "hidden" contraband. As if the strip search isn't humiliating enough. The officers are quick and efficient; soon we are dressed and in another line against the fence, waiting for the dogs.

Sniff, sniff, done. We then wait while some officers search the rooms and others rake the pebbles on the yard looking for hidden treasures. While we are waiting, I notice a sudden congregation right outside our room in front of the small closet that houses the plumbing between the rooms. The DW and ADW and finally, even the Warden of Perryville are all there. It wasn't until later that we learn they found two shanks in the closet. I am told they looked very old and the Powers decided they must have been left over from the days when men were housed here. Shanks are more a male thing. Women aren't so violent; they would rather gossip and tattle.

Soon the excitement is over, and we are locked back in our rooms. Lynn and I are speechless with joy. Our room has hardly been touched and only one pair of my orange sweatpants were thrown away because I had "cut" them shorter, so they would fit and not drag on the ground as I walked. Our pitiful treasures are all here. It doesn't take long before our beds are remade, our drawers arranged, and we're back to normal. We are hugely relieved. All those rumors of terror were just that, fuel to feed the fires of boredom. By dinner time, it is all over and we are free from the confines of the room. I come away a little wiser. I must stay away from the rumor mill and the inmate hysteria, no matter how seductive. Ignoring gossip is always a good idea ... *inside and out*.

Chapter 15...

Further Down The

Rabbit Hole

One of the biggest adjustments for me living behind the wires is the amazing variety of rules in each jail and prison. They're all different depending on the administration and the personality of its leaders. Some rules make perfect sense and are designed to protect everyone: staff and inmates alike. Others border on insanity and are designed to make inmates' lives as miserable as possible. They harken back to the old philosophy of warehousing prisoners and do little to encourage inmates to make decisions or learn how to be responsible. A professor told me there is logic in ADC's illogical pattern that helps to create an atmosphere of imbalance and confusion amongst the inmates.

One of the most important elements of stability behind bars is mail. It's the link to children, family, and friends. It's a symbol that someone values you as a human being and can go a long way toward influencing an inmate's future.

Inmates are not allowed to write to any inmates in any other prisons nationwide. No further contact is allowed. To write to other family members that are also incarcerated, you must prove that you're a spouse, sibling, or parent.

It's okay to live together for years, but no communicating afterwards. The theory is that we shouldn't have anything to do with felons or ex-felons, but with 1 in 100 people now behind bars, the field for friends becomes seriously limited. I've known women who weren't allowed to live at home because someone else in the family was an ex-felon. Instead of being allowed to parole to their home where their family and children live, and rent is free, they're forced to go to a half-way house where they must pay rent and where all the other residents are, you guessed it, ex-felons.

They even have the power to split up husbands and wives who've been married for years prior to their felony. This blanket policy is destructive, expensive, and cruel to enforce. But enforce it they do, often harshly. I knew a young woman released on parole that had a date with an ex-felon. It was a date, not a robbery or a murder or a DUI - a date. And where did she meet him? At her community service, filled with ex-felons. She had not committed a new crime. This is what is known as a technical violation of a parole rule. Her parole was revoked, and she was returned to prison for two years. Previously, this young woman had been a model inmate. No record of disciplinary problems or poor attitude. And upon release, she was not a troublemaker. So, let's charge the tax payer about $40,000 to punish her for a date.

Next on my list of draconian rules has to do with books. Earlier I mentioned inmates are only allowed to own seven books and five magazines. They say this extraordinarily restrictive policy is for security measures, but again I think the pros far outweighed the cons. I've yet to hear of anyone using a book for a weapon, although I know getting smarter is definitely a tool for a brighter future. This leaves me baffled. Education is not encouraged in Arizona. After all, in the late nineties, the Legislature ordered that inmates must pass eighth grade education. If they do, they can get ninety days knocked off their sentence. That is eighth grade, not twelfth, not GED - eighth grade. What good will that do anyone in finding a job? You can't even say, "Do you want fries with that?"

It costs an average of $20,000 annually to house an inmate in Arizona. That's tuition in a good university, yet we cut the state education budget and increase the budget for prisons. According to a 1997 report by the Center on Crime, Communities, and Culture at the Open Society Institute, inmates with at least two years of college education have a mere 10 percent re-arrest rate. In April 2001, Fortune magazine cited a study that explored three decades of prison college education; it found that every dollar spent on education resulted in $1.71 in reduced crime costs.

There is another idiotic rule related to books that leaves me shaking my head. Our rooms are supposed to be Spartan. No comfort or color allowed. We are allowed to keep our TV, clock, and fan on the shelf by our bed, and we each have a shelf for store snacks. Everything else goes in our only drawer, including clothes, coat, hat, hygiene, books, and program materials. The drawers are stuffed. Consequently, it is very hard to find and access things quickly. Even if there is space on the snack shelf, we are not allowed to keep our books there. Consider the person on the top bunk-ME. Every time I needed a book or study materials, I had to climb down, then up the ladder. It's ridiculous. I can keep the TV on the shelf, but not books.

Calendars are another mind-numbing issue. The store sells us an 8 x 11 all-on-one sheet calendar that is supposed to serve us to keep track of appointments, classes, medicines, visits, etc. Of course, there is no room to write on it, but in Wonderland, we're supposed to be responsible. Why then aren't inmates allowed to have a proper 12-month calendar or day timer with room to keep track of our lives? Families would love to send these in, but it is not allowed. Why? Because the store sells a calendar, period.

There's a *crazy clothes rule.* When I leave my room early in the morning and the temperature is 48° and drizzling, I'll wear my sweatshirt and coat. When I return from work at two o'clock in the afternoon, it is warm, but policy says I must wear my sweatshirt and coat regardless of the temperature. I cannot carry them. If I go to a visit when it's chilly and I wear my sweatshirt, I must keep it on no matter how much it warms up. They say it's a security risk. I sure hope the public feels safer.

Remember the *crazy magazine rule.* I can't tear out an article to send to a friend or a recipe to keep or a picture to put on my bulletin board. If I do, the magazine immediately becomes contraband.

Another uniquely ADC restriction is fruit. They are convinced if inmates can buy fruit or real fruit juice, we will all immediately be malting hooch. If that happens, why not punish the guilty rather than prevent the rest of us from enhancing our extremely limited diet. We are served a Kool-Aid-wanna-be at meals that is sickeningly sweet, and we are sold powdered, presweetened drinks from the store. The dietician had the gall to tell us it's as good as drinking real juice because it is fortified. I figured she was either a terrible dietician or a really good liar. Inmates can have all the chips, candy, and cookies they can afford, but nothing healthy is allowed. And yet, all this creates very obese inmates prone to diabetes and heart disease. So, what's worse, dealing with a few individuals who try to make hooch, or paying the costly medical bills related to the diseases caused by obesity?

Being proactive is rare in prison, especially with medical issues. The majority of the population has some problem with addiction. Drugs and alcohol are definitely forbidden, but another major addiction, smoking, is supported, mainly because the staff is addicted too. There's been a lot of talk about making the prison a non-smoking facility, but they're afraid if they do about a third of the staff will quit.

One of my real pet peeves is the crazy cigarette rule that I've mentioned before. I still have a hard time grasping these numbers. Inmates are allowed to buy ten packs of cigarettes, seven packs of chewing tobacco, and twenty-four pouches of rolling tobacco every week. They can buy twenty-four sodas, ten candy bars and ten bags of chips every week. But we aren't allowed to have healthy snacks. Do you see a pattern here? If you choose, you can smoke yourself to death. It's been asked to sell the patch to inmates to help them stop smoking, but got a resounding NO. I'm not trying to begrudge anyone their tobacco and candy, but I wish fruit and books were as readily available. It's a fact - healthy bodies and minds would cost ADC's Medical Department a lot less money in the long run.

Harvard Medical School and other researchers have shown the link between healthy bodies and healthy minds which even in prison could lead to more productive inmates who wouldn't re-offend. Yet, that proactive path is rarely followed. A prison Weight Watcher's program would make a huge impact, but first there would have to be healthy foods available. One Sunday morning's brunch consisted of a biscuit and a cinnamon roll, a ladle of gray gelatinous stuff called sausage gravy (I think the tiny specks were the sausage bits), one-half cup of fried potatoes, one boiled egg, one cup of cheerios, one-quarter cup of canned pineapple, and eight ounces of milk. If you ate all of it, you were guaranteed a food coma.

There are acres of fields surrounding most of ADC's prisons that used to be planted with crops. The prisons were self-sufficient, and vegetables were plentiful. That was stopped years ago, and now ADC pays out millions of dollars to an outside contractor to feed us terrible meals. Now we get a tissue thin slice of tomato at sixteen meals a year, we never see any kind of squash, and broccoli is very rare. Lots of potatoes though, and always with a weird taste.

ADC policies could fill a room. These are just a few of the nonsensical ones that do more harm than good. Usually I try to laugh them off, so I won't cry. My problem is I try to understand them, and ADC operates on the theory that ours is not to reason why. Don't ever question, just obey the rules. That's what an inmate does.

In the real world, people make decisions based on questions and evaluations, and then they take responsibility for their decisions. In prison, making decisions is rare, and yet very important for inmates to learn. A professor told me studies show the average person makes about 6,000 decisions a day; an average inmate makes about 600. When release comes, fear and confusion come with it because the outside world is just one huge Wal-Mart of choices and decisions. The key to surviving and thriving in all of this is patience and a sense of humor. Come to think of it, those qualities will go a long way anywhere ... *inside or out*.

Chapter 16...Attitude

I coined a new acronym - WIGO. It stands for When I Get out. When I Get Out I'm going to get a job. When I Get Out I'm going to be a blonde, I'm going to hug my dog, I'm going to Vegas and my life will be perfect. Isn't that just like outside? When I get a job, when I get a raise, when I get married, when I lose weight, then my life will be perfect. We're always waiting for LIFE to happen. We all have dreams, plans, and possibilities for our perfect future.

So, what do we do until all our dreams come true? A lot of inmates wish that, like Sleeping Beauty, they could take one huge sleeping pill at R & A (Receiving and Admitting) and wake up at the end of their sentence because freedom is the ultimate dream come true. A lot of people outside are like that too; people wishing their lives away. For many, they find numbness and escape in drugs. They literally sleepwalk through their lives. Whenever I ask what attracted them to drugs, nine times out of ten, its numbness.

Prison is a perfect example of wishing time away. Everyone has a different approach to doing time. First, there are the hardcore inmates who come in mad at the world and ready to fight at the drop of a hat. Their vision of life is from the streets - survival of the fittest, don't be a wimp, "I can lick you any day." They sit on the yards, rain or shine (in Arizona it's mostly shine), smoking, swearing, and criticizing what's wrong with the world, the prison, the officers, and the other inmates. They don't have any solutions, but they are world champs in criticizing.

Occasionally, they flex their muscles with a fight. With the men, it's usually a quick one round that the C.O.'s don't even see. With the women, it's more flailing of arms and hair-pulling with maybe a lucky bite or scratch. Everybody gets hauled off to The Hole to cool off for a week or two or, if it's serious, six months. One young woman spent the first two years of her prison life in The Hole with intermittent weeks of freedom in general population. Her anger was incredibly deep, and she was determined to be pissed off.

Outside there are people like that too, mad at the world. Mostly they sit in bars smoking and swearing and bitching about what's wrong with the world, their job, their boss, and their spouse. They won't make a move to change things, like maybe their attitude, but how they can moan. And just like inside, they even pick an occasional fight to feed their anger, determined to be pissed off too.

After the hardcore troublemakers, there are the time wasters. They don't fight. They don't even get in much trouble, but, oh, how they waste time. Somehow, they manage to avoid any idea of a job, sitting on their bunks, watching endless TV (bought with their families' hard earned cash).

There are also the champion card players, any game, anytime. The card players usually team up with the hard-core smokers. Smoke, TV, cards, the great prison and the great American pass times. Outside the same type of people wish their lives away, wasting time living by the WIGO creed: When I Get a job, a husband, a house, a new figure, my life will be perfect. Meanwhile, I'll just waste my time away with drugs or alcohol or video games or shopping.

Finally, there are those inmates who scurry to get a job, join programs, sign up for school, and go to church. I was that way. I worked a 40-hour week from eight in the morning until four in the afternoon as an assistant to Ms. Whitney, CO III. I'd stumble off my upper bunk at 6:30, splash water on my face, brush my teeth, make my instant coffee and slide into the dreaded orange outfit we came to hate. It was a killer pace, but I was determined to make the most of my time. In seven months, I accomplished more than most inmates do in years.

So, what's the big difference? It's that old Charles Swindoll quote again about attitude. In prison we aren't in charge of much. We're told when and how to do everything. It's nice to realize we can control something, something so important, so powerful it impacts our life, our family, our job, our community, even our world. Look how one terrorist's desire to kill, like Osama Bin Laden, can destroy so much and how one man's desire to forgive, like Nelson Mandela, can change a country.

Often people take drugs because they feel like they're nothing, nobody, with no hope, no future. That's a negative attitude. But think of the nobodies who've impacted the world. Mother Teresa, Martin Luther King, Jr., Corrie ten Boom, Helen Keller, Gandhi, Oprah - all nobodies with a positive attitude. The gunmen at Columbine High School tried to destroy a community with their attitude. The community has not allowed that. They too have attitude - strong, positive, faith-based attitude. Who are they? They're nobodies, but nobodies with the right attitude. It's the same with us. We're all nobodies, but with the right attitude, we too can make a difference. When you realize that, you'll take charge of your life and stop waiting for the WIGO creed to happen. Then you will be the one to make a difference whether you are ... *inside or out.*

Chapter 17....

Money in Prison

Money in prison has a meaning and value that is totally contrary to the real world. Inmates have jobs. Well, some do. Those that have jobs make a salary. There is even a store for shopping. And, like outside, they have expenses. That all sounds familiar, but that's where the familiarity stops. In prison, money takes on a whole new meaning.

ADC wants the public to believe every inmate has something productive to do with their time, but over the years more and more jobs have been taken away and now there are very few left of meaning. Inmates used to act as secretaries and clerks to help alleviate the over-worked staff. Now, however, inmates aren't even allowed to answer phones, make copies, or type. There even used to be a farm where inmates could learn agricultural husbandry and the prison could be self-sufficient in the dining rooms, but that was stopped years ago.

The list of approved jobs is very limited. The few jobs that let inmates use their brains are called clerks, Program Clerks, Women in Recovery clerks, State Issue and Store clerks,

Counselor clerks and Chaplain's clerks. There are also Teacher's Aides who do all the teaching while the civilian teachers supervise. These jobs total about forty on a yard with nearly 800 women. Everything else is manual labor, including the floor crew, kitchen workers, supply clerks, shower and pod porters, office porters, visitation porters, yard crew and outside landscaping. It all involves cleaning or in the case of yard crew, raking rocks. Yes, there really is a job to keep the rocks neat and tidy.

For all these jobs, pay ranges from 10 cents to 45 cents an hour. Gosh, who makes 45 cents? Must be the Teacher's Aids, right? Nope. They start at 30 cents. It's the floor crew. That requires skilled labor, but teaching doesn't, in ADC's mind anyway, although Teacher's Aid is the only job that requires a score of 12/9 on the scholastic admission's test.

There is also a limited amount of jobs that start at 45 cents and go up to $1 working in the Garment Factory, the Print Shop, or outside landscaping crews in townships around the prison, like Goodyear. And there is a tele-marketing company that pays minimum wage for a very select group of about two hundred of the 3,600 at Perryville. Those women are fortunate enough to build up a nest egg for their release.

I've had several jobs. Initially, I was a bathroom porter, but that only lasted a couple of weeks. I became then became a Counselor's clerk, a position I held for the remainder of my prison term. Nice job, pleasant atmosphere, and 30 cents an hour. ADC policy states that inmates are supposed to get a 5 cent an hour pay raise every six months until they reach the 50-cent ceiling.

The gist is, no one has any money. But why would an inmate need any money? Doesn't the prison provide everything? Sort of. As a new inmate, you get three T ~ shirts, two pair of trousers, three pair of socks, panties and bras, one winter jacket, one baseball cap, and one pair of boots. Also, two sheets, one lumpy pillow and pillow case (a luxury after the jail), two very thin towels, and three washcloths. That's called State Issue. And, after all, what else does a girl need?

ADC also allows sweatshirt and sweatpants for winter and shorts for summer, but you have to buy them. It's a pretty cold winter for the women who can't afford a sweatshirt and summers are beyond miserable without shorts. If you have no family or outside support, life is much more difficult, and the isolation increases one hundred fold.

Additionally, ADC allows inmates to purchase a pair of sneakers by Nike or New Balance at a captive cost of $48. A deal outside, but on an inmate's salary, it's pretty steep. The option is wearing the very stiff blister-maker work boots made in China. The yards are very spread out and we can walk miles in a day so understandably the first thing an inmate asks her family to do is send money to buy the sneakers.

ADC is supposed to replace worn out clothes quarterly, but generally you just get someone else's less worn, faded, holey orange stuff. Fortunately, ADC also sells new T-shirts and trousers as well as panties, bras, and socks. More reasons for money. Clothes wear out fast in prison, especially since we wear the same stuff every day. Our sheets and towels are only replaced if they look like Swiss cheese and we aren't allowed to buy extras. Owning four sheets and three or four towels would be just too much luxury.

That covers our whimsically named State Issue. But what about hygiene needs? Each inmate is issued one roll of tissue-thin toilet paper a week and if you run out, too bad. I did run out in R & A and, in my naivete, I went to the officer to ask for more. He paused, looked at me and snapped, "No."

I was stunned. After all, toilet paper is a pretty basic human need and we aren't a third world country.

"But what shall I do?" I implored.

He sneered as he looked down on me like I was an insect and raised his eyebrow, "It sucks to be you."

If you run out of toilet paper, we are allowed to buy Charmin at 74 cents a roll which adds up to about two and a half hours work at 30 cents an hour. We are also issued fifteen sanitary pads a month. If you need more or want tampax, they are for sale. Luckily for me I didn't have to worry about the need for sanitary supplies.

The State provides nothing else unless you are indigent. That means you have less than $12.00 a month in your inmate account. An indigent inmate gets a small amount of the poorest quality soap, deodorant, toothpaste, a comb, shaving cream and a razor replaced when you run out. Anything else is considered a luxury. If friends and family didn't help, you would do without chap sticks, vitamins, vaseline, hand lotion, eye drops, aspirin, band aids, conditioner, sunscreen, a hair brush, paper, a pen, stamps, envelopes, mouthwash, q-tips, the very basics that you take for granted on the outside. These are NOT state issue.

There are also luxuries, like a clock, a radio/DVD player, a TV, a stinger (heats water), a lamp, a few arts and crafts supplies, and the most important of all, an electric fan that cools your rooms down to 90 degrees in the summer and serves to dry both hair and clothes.

Chapter 18...

Compliments

Prison is not a place for compliments. I'm not sure why because a system that constantly criticizes and berates creates a person with low self-esteem and high anger. I often wonder how the officers are trained. I know that giving compliments is definitely not part of the curriculum.

Sadly, many inmates don't know how to compliment either. They almost uniformly enter prison with their self-esteem in the gutter. The only thing they're any good at is criticizing and judging. It's their life experience on their path to prison. They face drunken parents and drug-crazed boyfriends before they make it to angry cops, indifferent *public pretenders* (as the inmates call them) and not so indifferent judges. A compliment in prison is a rarity, priceless as a raisin would be if it suddenly appeared in our weekly bowl of com flakes.

I think it's just the desperation we feel inside, desperation for kindness, compassion, laughter, and a priceless compliment. A compliment can change so much with just a few words. Isn't it funny how we tend to discard them or refuse to acknowledge their worth? Practice giving compliments.

Yummy dinner.

I love your shirt.

Aren't you pretty?

You did a great job.

I appreciate you.

Chapter 19...

Punishment or Correction

I've started thinking about the purpose of prison. Is it to punish or to correct? In prison, the staff tells us they are not here to punish us. Our punishment is our separation from society. That is indeed a very big punishment. But why do I feel there is no correction?

On a day when the temperature has been about 112 degrees for many days, put on your heaviest polyester pants and t-shirt, go out in your garage with a very small fan, and spend the day. Have lunch there, soup (yes, soup) and a bologna sandwich. Sweep, mop and clean, watch TV, read. Try to nap on a plastic cot, eat a lukewarm dinner, and spend the night. This is Arizona prison in the summer.

Summer lasts nearly four months, 1440 minutes a day of sheer, unrelenting, blast furnace heat. I arrived late August, 2009 so you can imagine. The small bit of grass on the field chokes and turns brown. The few prized trees are gasping and pitiful. Looking forlorn, the pigeons wander into the community showers to drink the stagnant water pooling on the hot concrete. The prairie dogs wisely burrow underground.

The prison yards on Perryville are very spread out. We walk everywhere, blocks and blocks between buildings. No shade. The administration offices and classrooms are air-conditioned, but that's it. Evaporative coolers slog away to cool the cells and cafeterias. They work until the temperature hits 90 degrees. After that, the cells become concrete coffins of heat. There is no relief.

They've actually done studies that show evaporative coolers are environmentally inefficient and costly. They use more power and water than air-conditioning, but ADC keeps repairing the thirty year old coolers, knowing nobody cares about inmates and their health. In Arizona, it is a health issue. There is more heat exhaustion than I can count, and in 2009 a 48 year old inmate was left outside in a holding cell for four hours in triple digit heat. The holding cell was only 20 yards from a staffed control room where the correctional officers should have been watching her. It ends up costing money in Medical attention. One way or another, the tax payer pays.

Let's get back to your garage. What can you do in your stifling garage to relieve the heat? You can't go to the fridge for an ice cold coke. You can buy a 10 pound bag of ice for $2.24, about a day's salary if you are lucky enough to make 30 cents an hour. For another $1.35, you can buy a very small, thin Styrofoam cooler to keep the ice in. The ice melts in a few hours, but meanwhile, you can have ice cold water, and that is a luxury. You can also wet down your shirt and head. That helps. You can wear a wet washcloth around your neck You can fill an old hair spray bottle with water and spray yourself continuously, sort of like the misters at an outdoor cafe. That's pretty much it. Even the showers are scalding. No relief there, not anywhere.

Punishment is much higher on the list than rehabilitation and America's prisons are designed to punish. Many people think that inmates don't deserve more than two or three cups of water a day and a rancid washcloth. What does that teach? It certainly doesn't teach a person to be kind or considerate. It does, however, teach inmates that they are worthless, disposable human beings.

Before prison, I was a confident woman. Prison ate away at my confidence. I was always afraid and wondered what had happened to my confidence? I realized then just how much prison had affected me. It is a Chinese water torture of denigration, and if I was affected so dramatically, imagine what it does to others lacking confidence.

In the end, it boils down to humanity. Is this who we really are? Are we a nation that prefers to punish in such dehumanizing ways? Are we really teaching people a lesson? What we are doing is treating people so badly that they become bitter, angry, and mean, completely unprepared for a life of civility and respect.

I learned other things in prison. I learned that everyone wants love, but many in prison have never had it, from parents, friends, or partners. Prison is full of horror stories. We have become a nation of fear and anger. We'd rather flex our muscles than flex our hearts. Love seems to always have conditions.

I could make this really long, detailing what we need to do, but we all know; we're just not doing it. Be kind, be considerate, be respectful, stop judging. Open our hearts. Think about others first.

Chapter 20...

Telephones

Aren't telephones wonderful? This tiny, miraculous instrument connects you with everyone important in your life- parents, children, spouse, etc. I wonder if Alexander Graham Bell knew he was creating an instrument that would connect the world.

Telephones gradually found their way into every room in the house. They came in a rainbow of colors and shapes. Remember the Princess phone? The Mickey Mouse phone? Then the cell phone revolution hit and our lives were changed forever. Now people walk around with tiny phones seemingly glued to their heads. Everyone has a phone, even kids in grammar school. Everyone except inmates.

Prison is designed to separate inmates from the world. Some prisons do that better than others. ADC is an expert in separation. We are very limited in who we are allowed to call- only the same ten people who are on the inmate's visitation list. The process for approval is lengthy and time consuming. First, the inmate sends the application to the friend or family member who wants to visit. The applicant must return the completed form to the Visitation Officer for processing. It then takes ADC about two months to run background checks for approval. Bear in mind that the inmate can spend up to three months in R & A waiting for a bed in general population.

Outside in the free world, you are too often tied to your cell phone and just wish it would stop ringing. Inside, inmates know that connections are precious. The ability to communicate over that visionary instrument created by Mr. Bell is priceless and you only realize it when it's taken away. Connections are a good thing, keeping us motivated, encouraged, and loved, things we all need ... *inside or out.*

Chapter 21...

Judgment

There are hundreds of women at Santa Maria. Many share the experience of abuse, others are addicts. Most have experienced the horrors of Estrella J ail. We've all been judged by the courts and society. There is a broad common bond of sorrow, pain and grief, and yet we cannot get along. Sometimes, the race to judgment and the lack of compassion take my breath away.

I first noticed it at Estrella where everyone is the same, all dressed in those hideous black and white stripes, sticky and sweaty in the heat. The conditions are hostile; the guards are demeaning; the atmosphere is dark and heavy. The lines of division are obvious. It is 'them' vs. 'us'. We are all sisters, sharing a common grief, but we can't get even that right. We are a dysfunctional family, pathetic lost souls with little idea how to come together in compassion.

We've all been in court, listening to prosecutors tell their version of the truth. They paint the defendants with a broad brush of darkness while the defense brings in their brush of light. Somewhere in the middle is the truth, a human being encompassing both dark and light, neither as dastardly nor as pure as painted in court.

Nevertheless, knowing this, the Judge picks up his brush and adds to the canvas of despair. We are judged and no one likes it. You have to stand there and keep your mouth shut, even when it is unfair and unbalanced; even when you lose your job, your family, your dignity and your freedom. You are judged and you hate it.

That same day, upon return to the jail, you pick up where the judge left off. Addicts judge thieves who judge prostitutes. They all judge child abusers who are considered the lowest of the low in prison. It's a twisted pride of 'my crimes are not as bad as yours.' But we're all here for a crime, all judged by society and staff. What is it about human nature that takes such glee in judging?

When I left the jail and got to the prison yard at Perryville, I found the judging was here too, but I could go to my cell and escape it. Most of the chatter went on in the smoking section over card games, and I wasn't a part of that. The cell was small, but it was a sanctuary that kept the negativity at bay.

Before being moved to my cell, I was surrounded by women in a dorm where the neighbors are only two feet away. There is simply no escape. We are stacked up like boxes on a shelf and we hear everything. One day, I was washing my hands in the bathroom when an argument started between two women. It was loud but brief, ending sharply when one called the other a fucking whore. I expected there to be blows, but the one being attacked turned quickly and walked away. She had five weeks left on her sentence and didn't want to do anything to jeopardize that.

The name calling is common here. Sometimes I learn what triggers it; sometimes I don't.

It's never earth shattering or even deserved. It's a quick judgment, a typical knee-jerk reaction. I feel so sad when people don't look into my heart to see how much I care. Yet, by judging others, I'm refusing to look into their hearts. What is the drive behind their behavior, their anger, their kindness, or their cruelty? That is always my challenge and my opportunity. Prison is the perfect place to practice, a sort of crash course in Compassion

101. I want to graduate before release. After all, seeing into the hearts of others is a priceless ability, one we can all use.

Chapter 22...

The Elephant in the Room

One of the greatest unknowns about prison and certainly one of the most frightening is the strip search. I wasn't going to write about it, but then I realized it's the elephant in the room and cannot be ignored.

I had my first strip search upon entering Estrella Jail when I changed from my street clothes to the infamous black and white stripes chosen to add extra humiliation to the whole jail experience. I was in a total daze. I'd been crammed into a twelve foot by twelve foot holding tank with about thirty-six other women. I'd been given a tiny bit of unidentifiable food, but I couldn't and didn't want to eat.

Now a grumpy officer was telling me to strip for her and numbly I complied. Carefully, I folded my beige capri pants and sheer blouse. (When would I ever see them again?) Then I learned there is a proper routine for a strip search. Starting at the top, first you open your mouth widely so she can see that you aren't hiding drugs.

Then, you lean forward and show behind your ears after which you flip your hair to show nothing is hiding there. Most of the women have very long hair.

Next, I had to spread my toes and show her the bottoms of my feet. Finally, she told me to squat and cough three times and, while I was bent over, I was told to spread my cheeks of my derriere. She didn't call it that though. I suppose this is the ultimate humiliation. I suppose it is the vulnerability. I always feel vulnerable in my nakedness, and if the officer is hostile it makes it worse. It must be a bit like rape. Rape is the ultimate degradation for any woman, when she feels completely and utterly helpless and vulnerable. I've never been raped but close to it at one point. Many of the women in prison had been and they talk about it casually to gloss over the pain, but I wondered if the strip search brings back that pain, the fear and the helplessness.

All the inmates who work off the yard are stripped every day, just in case they are trying to smuggle in something. Since I didn't work off site, I was spared that. The strip is bad enough, but the strip shack is freezing in the winter and broiling in the summer, just to add injury to insult.

Inmates are also stripped after every visit in case some visitor has tried to smuggle in God knows what-usually drugs, but since Perryville is a woman's prison, lip-gloss and perfume samples are more likely.

I am grateful for my visits from my family every weekend and try to zip through the strip as quickly as possible. After every visit, four inmates at a time go into a classroom and stand between long tables that are positioned at tall angles to create dividers and a semblance of privacy. The officers can see the inmates; the other inmates can't see each other. I know the drill. Strip off your clothes, place on the chair, and wait for the C.O. Start at the top ... aahh, flip, squat, cough, spread, and dress, done.

Life is about choices. I made choices that took me to prison and I made choices every day while I was there, choices to maintain my sanity, my dignity, my humanity. It was not easy. Some days I felt lonely, some days I felt afraid, some days I cried. But every day I made the choice to stand up straight and walk tall. It's good to remember we all have a choice ... *inside and out.*

Chapter 23...

Resolution

"My New Year revolution is I ain't eatin' no more cake," another inmate announced when she sat at the breakfast table. "This shit makin' me fat."

"Resolution," I corrected her.

"Wha? That's the name of this shit?" she asked as she directed her spork at it.

"No, it's New Year's resolution.   As in resolve, like make up your mind. Not revolution."

"I always said revolution."

"Well, you were wrong," I told her bluntly.

"Don't matter.   I just ain't eatin' no cake. After today," she said with her mouth full of the brown stuff.

"Good luck with that," I snorted. Perryville serves cake with everything: cake with bologna, cake with meatloaf. Sometimes cake was the entire meal itself. The prison served so much cake that you'd think Marie Antoinette was the warden.

"What the difference between resolution and what you called it?"

"You called it revolution."

"Yeah. What the difference?"

I had to stop and think because many inmates have never done the right thing in their lives. Resolving to do one thing better – or one thing differently – is a revolution for them. I debated whether I should even venture into this philosophical 'hood.

"Well, it's just that when you resolve to do something, you are in control. Revolution means change, but in a different way for New Year's. Resolution means decision..." And before I realized it, it came out of that place in my face that takes the cake. "... more than the actual changing."

Except for her 'revolution' I hadn't witnessed one other inmate voice a New Year's resolution. Maybe it's because they had no intention of changing. Maybe they didn't know how to change. Most likely is that they didn't know that that they could.

Anyone can decide to change at any time, but we choose to change at New Year's because of the fresh start that changing one or two digits on your paperwork provides. At the New Year, books close on old ways. On January 1st, we bow to calendars and expect that opening a new one means opening a new self. I don't see how anyone wrung by criminal justice could ever feel like she has a clean slate on any day, especially New Year's. You have to be on the Chaplain's short list just to get a calendar in there. They run out quickly.

Any inmate lives in her mistakes. They may not be criminal errors. Perhaps all they are is bad judgment. Every mistake surrounds you in the cement walls, the two inch mattresses, the crappy cake, the smell of antiseptic dirt in every building, the guards who called us "job security" because they predict we will recidivate when we leave the facility, never changing. Everyone else gets to reset, reboot and reinvent themselves at the end of December. We never really get that chance.

Inmates promise to change all the time. They make at least an oral decision not to come back to jail, not to 'pick up' (start using drugs), to take care of their kids. But the resolution finds dilution when they need to do something.

The one thing they do is make change by throwing out their stuff. They throw out everything they own in the prison: papers, toiletries, pictures, even t shirts and underwear, cleaning the slate like an employee being fired does to an abusive boss' desk. Whoosh.

No matter how I protested: "*Wait! You'll need those receipts! Whoa, whoa, whoa...how are you going to change your underwear?*" they proceed. At first I thought it was mania or anger but after watching them clean slate, I understood. It was the only way to start fresh.

Of course, clean slates that come about like this don't stay that way. Chaos ensues when the slater begs everyone else for hair conditioner or cries to me that she needs to return something to commissary but doesn't have proof that she bought it. It's like erasing a whiteboard only to see the colored scribble lines you just wiped away still show but now they're just white. You never get clean.

Without any resolution, the New Year's celebration amounted to certain women kicking their doors and walls at midnight when they watched the ball drop in Times Square. My first new years in the dorms, one room housing 10 women, inmates couldn't compartmentalize the party so I watched the melee from my bottom bunk. Strip shows by chunky dancers doing the worm on the filthy floor, lap dances. Then women tore their inmate handbooks into confetti and tossed it around the dorm at midnight celebrating the fact that one year had passed and another one was coming. At 12:05 AM those same women sat on their bunks and cried that one year had passed and another year was coming.

Feeling the passage of time is essential to survival in prison. It's also what kills you. When you are in prison you can't have your cake and eat it too. In fact, since you made a mistake, you can't have it at all, unless it's served on a plastic prison tray.

Chapter 24...

Dooker Lookers

My father told me never to shit where I eat. I couldn't take the advice in there because I lived in a bathroom. It happened to include a bunk bed for the bathroom's two inhabitants but it is a 9 x 12 foot bathroom with a counter where I ate, prepared snacks, write, and folded clothes.

I once refused to poop in public bathrooms like those in restaurants, stores and rest areas. The stalls never afford enough privacy and the sounds and smells always travel.

The habit would have broken itself when I saw the prison cells. If my cellmate and I were locked in together, I poop exactly one yard away from her. Then we switch places.

If pooping right in someone's face were not embarrassing enough, a window in every cell door allows the guards to see us on the toilet. Safety and security, the catch-all excuse for any violation of prisoner rights, allows them to see in to see that we are alive, not fighting, un-escaped and possibly mid-turd.

Every time I needed to poop, I went to the door and look to see if either guard's tour of the unit is impending. If I saw him coming, I held it until he's gone. I would rather suffer abdominal pain than endure the humiliation that I did when I was sitting on the toilet as one of the guards whom I respect circuited my tier.

"Mr. Smith, I'm on the toilet. Can you stay away from the door?" I should have been embarrassed just by being caught hanging a rat but instead my extreme vanity took over. *Does this toilet make my ass look fat?* I wondered because that was a vision of myself I hadn't experienced yet; we have only 4 x 5 inch mirrors and a reflection of the toilet – and my ass – could never fit in those tiny rectangles.

Another time, when my cell held up the far end of the yard and it was futile to look out my door's window to catch an upcoming tourist guard, an officer who was delivering a Chrono from the CO backed into my room while speaking to another inmate. I was peeing, mid-stream, when he walked fully into my cell, a big no-no. He should have turned and left when he realized that he had walked in on me in flagrante but instead he froze, staring at me as if he never knew that women in the facility peed occasionally. The freeze lasted a few seconds too long.

"Sir... you need to leave," I had to remind him. I had already bunched my toilet paper and was poised to go in for the wipe. He could have placed the Chrono on the bed or even kept it with him until another delivery round but instead he dropped it directly on the floor where he stood. He seemed almost angry, as if it were my fault that I expel liquid waste.

Usually the CO's get pissed about catching women on the commode only when they believe that the inmate is purposefully exposing herself to him. For the most part, the open-toilet policy forces the guards to treat poop as what it is: an inescapable part of incarceration, the true-life version of getting the shitty end of the stick.

Some low-lying wall that exposed her face and torso yet blocked an inmate's lower half when she sits on the toilet would not so disrupt the order of the facility that we shouldn't have them in all of our cells. It's true that people and things hide easily behind barricades, but the prison allows little partitions to protect the new admissions to the prison in their cells in the inpatient medical unit. If little dividers work safely in these rooms, then they shouldn't be dangerous in other cells. I guess that, because new admissions to prison are famous for the incessant puking and diarrhea associated with heroin withdrawal, the guards probably petitioned for the walls in that housing unit to censor the more grizzly scenes.

I assume that the guards think that the rest of us don't need the walls because once a prisoner has been here for a year, she develops a routine that limits her exposure time in her lavatory and her exposure time to him. Of course, a few depraved guards are known to like to catch the inmates on the toilet, but those degenerates are rare as well as well-marked; inmates warned each other when one of them worked in our yard.

Humiliation seems to account for an unreasonable proportion of rehabilitation in there. Remedies for the ill-behaved must include humility, for sure, but not necessarily degradation, which is what public pooping is for me. Surely, the male guards know that even women who want to become ladies take an occasional shit.

The open squat policy is bad because so many women in this facility struggle with boundaries. Some, like me, wanted walls all the way around them; we never feel safe unless ramparts surround us. Others have no shame and no control on how much they expose; they flash the guards, detail gynecological issues to strangers and expect other inmates to feel equally comfortable when they prance around naked or hug them from behind, by surprise. Every time the facility erases yet another border around acceptable behavior, the exhibitionists' confusion only grows and the inhibited inmates like me end up feeling violated.

Chapter 25...

By Any Other Name

"I am not a number!" Number Six would protest on the 1960's television show "The Prisoner."

Number Six's remains a chronic inmate complaint – we're not numbers, we're people, known by names – and Number Six was right; no inmate is a number. We are now six numbers, strings of digits and dashes that each new inmate earns in 'Receiving & Admitting,' the prisoner delivery dock.

Instead, staff members use our last names as our only names. I learned during my first days there.

Women there bitch that this practice depersonalizes us. But I always understood the reason behind using last names to be that there were too many Heather's or Maria's there and when a C/O yelled that name, too many heads turned; the last name narrowed the field a little bit.

Because of the guards' usual practice of referring to us by our last names, prisoners conclude that when guards call an inmate by her first name, they mean it as a sign of respect. I don't know if that's even possible in there. But, if calling an inmate by her first name is respectful, that would be something we need to avoid, so I was Stearns.

Prison is a culture of insult and the fact that these institutions collect the flawed among us makes nicknaming people easy. Male or female facility, there's always a "Red," a "Slim" and a "Tiny" in prison. I think it might be against the law for a prison not to have a Red, a Slim or a Tiny living within.

The remaining nicknames zero in on weaknesses and turn the general population into one giant bully. The women dubbed one inmate with a congenitally malformed arm "Chicken Wing." The rest are no kinder: "Cry Baby" for a woman taken to tears, "Fatty Girl" for the obvious, "Teen Wolf" for a woman stricken with thick, dark facial hair from polycystic ovary disease, "Green Eyes" for everyone whose eyes are neither dark brown nor black.

We fill out the rest of the roster with some cutesy names: a "Gucci," a "Smiley," a "Gypsy".

There are a couple of "Rock Stars" but those are always self-imposed. Anyone who was from the south is called "Country". I didn't say the names were accurate.

I suppose some psychological theory would explain the reliance on nicknames in a prison: that people need to become someone else in order to metamorphosis or rehabilitate themselves, that the nickname shields their true identities and feelings from discovery by others, a self-imposed protective layer of depersonalization. If all we're known by is our names, then changing them changes our impact on the world. Or so we hope.

But after living there for 8 months, I doubt that the reason for nicknames is as complex as my theory. Nicknames in prison are just accessible words that lend themselves to caste-making, to power. Nicknames aren't funny monikers we use to refer to friends with affection; they're oppressive classification. Weak, disfranchised people will do almost anything for a little bit of power, to feel a little bit better about their stations in life, so they call a woman with high cheekbones "Skeletor," thinking it will change something for Skeletor or her bully when it won't.

Always an overachiever and coming from a background of abundance, I had several nicknames in there. They were "Tinkerbell", "Cinder" (short for Cinderella because I was always cleaning something), and "Mighty Mouse", because of my small stature and the fact that I have helped an inmate here and there with written endeavors. *"Here I come to save the day!"* they sing and raise their right arms high, palm out, though, not in a fist like the real Mighty Mouse. Not making a fist is a switch in here.

"Put that down!" I tell them and they think its humility speaking but they're wrong. The raised arms smack too much of the Nazi salute for my comfort.

"Smiley" and the others still didn't understand because, to prisoners, any name is better than a number.

Chapter 26...

"Go Shorty, It's My Birthday"

How was dinner? Sometimes the C/O's ask when you stroll back to your housing unit after a meal, a little incredulous that anyone actually ate what was served.

I shrugged.

"Okay. I always want chili in 100 degree heat. I only went because tomorrow's my birthday and the meals are worse."

"Tomorrow's your birthday, Stearns? Doin' anything fun? Havin' a party?" he joked. That's always a knee-slapper to them."

I climbed up on my bunk and lay, frozen still, so that the 5-watt fan could chill the sweat all over me; rooms without air conditioning and small fans aren't fun in 100-degree weather. For a woman to celebrate a birthday in prison is about as pathetic as it gets.

"Smiley" poked her head into my cell.

"Hey, Rosa has a question for you, so come out when you can," she said.

I walked out to the yard and found a party, a huge, unexpected one. A banner made from 20 pieces of contraband copy paper. Women on the tier had made personal pizzas for everyone – 15 in total – by smashing sour cream and onion chips with cheese and hot water and spreading the mix between two tortillas to make a crust. Rice and beans.   Ramen noodles made into spaghetti. Chicken salad wraps. Tuna casserole. Individual cakes made of honey buns mushed up with brownies and cappuccino to make a bread pudding, frosted with Fluff and topped with M&M's.

My mother would have fallen into a wilted heap herself if this had ever been served at the parties she had for me, but these dishes were prison's go-all-out gourmet.

They had to start days ago and not one person wasn't involved with the planning.

"You did this for me?" I was still taking it in.

"You do a lot for us," Rosa said as she mixed Nestea for everyone.

I couldn't even react, mostly because the heat deflated me, but also because I was so touched by getting a surprise party for my birthday. I may not like the way my wishes are delivered, but even through all of these trials, I still get what I want.

Chapter 27...

In Low Places

To say that I'm better than the other inmates? That isn't true. To say that I'm just like them? That's a lie.

And most of them know it, too. The differences pop out in questions and fascination that turns me into an exhibit.

Friends and family plan in jail.

"You ever live in a motel?"

"No."

"You got a license for a car?"

"You mean to drive? Yes."

"You ever been on Food Stamps? Your fridge always stocked up, I bet."

"No... I guess."

"What kinda car you drive?"

"Why?"

"Your family decorate their house all nice, Victorian and shit up in there?"

"Ummm..."

Still, I called them friends and they returned the label. I got along with the other prisoners; I'd even say I had the least conflict with others of all the long-termers. When I first got out, I got one or two letters from "friends" that were still incarcerated, but not more than that. And that's why the term friend gets redefined for me in there. The only thing over which I can relate to other women over is that place and the fact that we were both there at the same time.

Connection.

I bonded with them when I was drowning and whirling in melodramatic victimization, thinking that my life is harder than other prisoners' paths. I could connect with them only when I go to some low places, emotional nadirs. If friendship must be borne of equal standing, it was the only way I could get there.

Sure, I wasn't denied much of anything in my life but I know what it's like to feel pressured to live up to impossible standards. *I've been through a lot of shit, too, you know! More than you!* Only when I started thinking that way could I feel like I was not unreachable in there.

But if I counted my blessings and humbled myself, I ended up valuing my sociological singleness a little too much and my feelings for the other women drew a little too close to pity. Sympathy brings distance. If it doesn't, then it's empathy. And if I empathized with them, then I have to admit that I'm like them. When I'm not. Except for the times that I am, like when I was there.

A library's worth of literature has been destroyed in this prison because women cram books between the corners of the cell doors and the jambs to keep them open. It was a scholastic Webster's, one with red linen covers that had been ripped off through years of cell cleaning, not overuse by injuring inmates. This is another thing that separates me from the others: I think books are for reading. That's the last thing that so many of the others will do with them.

"You can't use a dirty T-shirt or something else? You're destroying and ripping the cover of ...what is this?...The Secret Lives of Bees. You're ruining the bees' secret lives. You are killing the bees," I told the first cellmate who did it in front of me. She didn't care about the bees, the book or bond that we could never have.

I might have looked up 'amity' or 'unity' but those letters had fallen away from the dictionary due to repetitive cell cleaning. I was lucky to find 'F' intact to look up 'friendship.' I won't even say how bad my life must have been that I had to look up this word at age 38 and get pissed off when I found: "the state of being friends."

Up a few lines, 'friend' informed me that the women I called friends were people "whom one knows and with whom one has a bond of mutual affection." Basically, someone you know and like – and who likes you back – is your friend.

But that's not true. Friendship is more than affection because; face it, that shit's temporary. Not just for their sake, but for yours, prison friends have to leave each other behind, leave each other there. Only the disconnect can save you both.

Chapter 28...

Pretty Little Liars

There are a million explanations for the fibs: mental illness, denial of who they are or what they've done, escaping their current reality, trying to manipulate other people. It doesn't take more than freshman psych to jot down a well-informed list.

Many women will soon be called on their double-dealing – referred to as "bipolar" even though they're not – and ostracized as much as a group of prisoners can ostracize a woman with whom the state forces them to live with within 500 square yards.

I wasn't ostracized for my lie because most other inmates have rarely experienced the kind of consistency and relatively gentle nature I displayed when I helped them write letters, edited their schoolwork and helped them complete judicial forms. These activities made me a good, nice person to them.

"You're so nice. You're like an angel, like Jesus the way you help people in here," Debra told me.

"If you only knew ... " I replied and she smiled and nodded. I believe she interpreted my words to mean something like *If you only knew all the good I've done in my life...* but I meant was *Angel? Jesus? Me? No fucking way.* My water always stayed water.

Before landing in prison, I literally fell apart; I mean in two pieces. The nice person in me showed up when things were going well. The darker angel of my nature appeared whenever my fortune took a dive or whenever I was using drugs. I swore at people, made fun of them behind their backs and generally spewed nastiness at everyone because something bad was happening to me. Bad things happen to good people, but truly good people remain good and behave properly throughout the duration of the bad things. I thought that hitting a bad patch after my divorce excused me from having to comport myself with civility, mercy and kindness like all good people do.

Being mistreated by my ex-husband and his friends gave me leeway to lash out, at least in my mind, but I was lying to myself, pathologically. As a result, people around me never knew what to expect from me. *Was her kindness a lie? Does that explain why she just insulted me and called me a fucking idiot?* People avoided me and the further isolation made me angrier and entitled me to more explosions. I was vicious and this was my cycle. Prison, quite frankly, was probably the only place that would reform me, the spaces between the bars acting like a mirror serving the ugliness of my behavior right back to me.

Initially, I was too scared to lash out at others here in prison because guards had so much more power than I did, inmates so much more experience than I. Silently, though, I convinced myself that I had every right -and probably even an obligation – to tell the staff who were so undereducated (despite the fact that many have college diplomas and a handful have advanced degrees) and inmates what I really thought of them, but I didn't have time to do it. I was preparing to leave any day and leave them behind.

Then I sat with some nurse for a routine health screening. She knew my social and educational background.

"So, Stearns, what are you going to do while you're here?"

"Nothing. I'm not going to be here long."

"But if you are here for a while ... your sentence is long," she posed to me.

"Even if I am here for a while, there's nothing here for me ... "

"What about tutoring?" she asked me.

"No. There's nothing here for me. You can't really be stupid enough to think I would tutor inmates," I said, my words sounding like those of the haughty bitch in an after-school special. When I said them, the words seemed well-bred and tactful to me.

Everyone warns against the perils of self-hatred; "Don't say that!" people chant around the person who says he hates himself. But, at that moment in the prison nurse's office, I loathed myself. And for the insufferable effrontery I showed, I should have hated myself; my self deserved to be despised. It was through detesting myself on that hot miserable day on a molded plastic chair, slippery from endless friction with the asses of other self-loathers that made me realize I needed punishment and rehabilitation to rid myself of the parts I hated. It's like I knew a revolution needed to happen and I knew it needed to happen in there.

Confinement reveals false life stories because it unifies personalities; that's what it did to me. You are who you are in prison and you can never be someone else and I don't speak of identity theft. Those women who Jekyll-and-Hyde everyone at home – self-described angels who are really nasty ghouls who heckle and hide – must pick one persona and go with it. Eventually all fake life stories get abandoned, if not by their tellers then by the people around them who know they're full of shit. It is what it is.

In prison, you need to decide who you are and then be that woman because she's the only human being who will carry you through your time. It's the one aspect of rehabilitation in which incarceration never fails: developing a type of self-reliance, even as one lives as a ward of the state. Being pulled out of society and out of your own cloud of lies lets you know how alone you really are and how the only one who can really fix you is you.

The way I got fixed was that I realized you can say you're something for a long time but, eventually, you have to be it. Thinking and proclaiming that I was a decent person was a really nice verbal billboard but eventually I had to deliver the goods.

Prison isolates a woman from everything and everyone she knew but isolation is not without its perks. Often women isolate themselves willingly to achieve peace and reflection through meditation because introspection never happens in a crowd. I doubt that l would have attempted to answer the questions that plagued me, like why I value the elusive goal of having everyone like me. As a free bird, I never asked myself why I'll screw up my own endeavors to help someone who really needs to carry her own cross. Why must I be right all of the time? Why do I care so much what others think of me? Am I skinny enough? And when I am right why do I care so much if others still think I'm wrong? Could, as friends suggest, hate really mask jealousy? Before I came to prison, the amount of self-esteem I had was pretty little so I couldn't and wouldn't answer these questions. I haven't locked in my responses as final, but while I was there, I started to formulate truthful responses to myself. It's about time.

Eight years ago I was released from Perryville Women's prison in Goodyear, Arizona. It was a beautiful March day. I was up at 3:30 in the morning....The release process included a lot of anxious waiting. I had my photo taken for my Identification Card I was given prior to my release. Went over last minute paperwork and lastly...given a check for the balance on my inmate account. I was handed a paper sack which contained my clothes that were brought by my friend Paul when he arrived to pick me up. I changed and was instructed to wait on a bench in an area just near the gates outside.

Finally, around 10:00 am, the chain link gates slid open and I walked out, free, into the welcoming arms of my brother, niece, nephew, Paul and my dog Roxy.

It was the most wonderful day I had in a very long time. Seeing my family made me realize what really matters in life...*inside or out*!

www.ingramcontent.com/pod-product-compliance
Lightning Source LLC
Chambersburg PA
CBHW030808180526
45163CB00003B/1188